REVOLUTION REJECTED

1775-1776

CANADIAN HISTORICAL CONTROVERSIES

Series Editor

W. J. ECCLES

Department of History, University of Toronto

FORTHCOMING TITLES

The Bourgeoisie in New France
Historiography of New France
The War of 1812
Rebellion in Upper Canada
English Attitudes and British North America: 1827-1849
Confederation
Canadian-American Relations: 1903-1914
The Winnipeg Strike
The Depression

p
♣
h

CANADIAN HISTORICAL CONTROVERSIES

Series Editor
W. J. ECCLES
Department of History, University of Toronto

REVOLUTION REJECTED

1775-1776

GEORGE A. RAWLYK

Department of History
Queen's University, Kingston, Ontario

PRENTICE-HALL OF CANADA, LTD.
Scarborough, Ontario

PRENTICE-HALL, INC., ENGLEWOOD CLIFFS, NEW JERSEY
PRENTICE-HALL INTERNATIONAL, INC., LONDON
PRENTICE-HALL OF AUSTRALIA, PTY., LTD., SYDNEY
PRENTICE-HALL OF INDIA, PVT., LTD., NEW DELHI
PRENTICE-HALL OF JAPAN, INC., TOKYO

Library of Congress Catalog Card No. 68-16528
78064-Pa
78065-C1
1 2 3 4 5 72 71 70 69 68
PRINTED IN CANADA

Contents

Series Editor's Preface

The aim of this series is to compare and to subject to critical scrutiny, the ways in which historians have treated major issues in Canadian history. Each volume defines one issue in space and time, and indicates its importance for both the people concerned and later generations. Selected quotations from contemporary sources indicate the views of the people of the period; then, the historians' interpretations of the issue are given and discussed critically. Finally, the author indicates what needs to be done, pointing out, wherever possible, evidence not yet utilized or inadequately examined by earlier historians, and suggests new lines of approach that could place the issue in a more revealing light.

It is hoped that in this way the student of history will gain, not only a better understanding of the events, but also an insight into the way in which history is written. He will, it is hoped, become aware that there is no such thing as "definitive history," that the history of this country was not brought down the mountain engraved on ten stone tablets by certain eminent scholars whose opinions cannot be questioned. Events in a historian's own time influence the way in which he views the past, the questions he asks of it, the methods he employs in seeking the answers, and the values that govern his judgements. Thus, what the historian has written has continually to be subjected to critical examination and his interpretations qualified or revised.

If this series enables those interested in the history of Canada to approach it more critically, with a better appreciation of what has been done, and a clearer idea of what needs to be done, it will have served its purpose.

W. J. E.

ACKNOWLEDGEMENTS

The author is indebted to the following publishers and authors for permission to reprint material included in this book:

Canadian Historical Association *Report* for "The Struggle for the New England Form of Township Government in Nova Scotia" by D. C. Harvey; Carnegie Endowment for International Peace for *Les Canadiens Français et leurs voisins du sud* by G. Lanctôt; Columbia University Press for *The Neutral Yankees of Nova Scotia* and *North Atlantic Triangle* by J. B. Brebner; Les Editions Fides and F. Ouellet for *Histoire économique et sociale du Québec 1760-1850*; Longmans Canada Limited for *Colony to Nation* by A. R. M. Lower; The Macmillan Company of Canada Limited for *The Empire of the St. Lawrence* by D. G. Creighton; *The New England Quarterly* and M. W. Armstrong for "Neutrality and Religion in Revolutionary Nova Scotia"; *The New England Quarterly* and Viola F. Barnes for "Francis Legge, Governor of Loyalist Nova Scotia, 1773-1776"; Oxford University Press for *The Quebec Act: A Study in Statesmanship* by R. Coupland; Progress Books for *The Founding of Canada Beginnings to 1815* by S. Ryerson; Dr. Marcel Trudel for *Louis XVI, Le Congrès Américain et le Canada 1774-1789*; University of Minnesota Press and A. L. Burt for *The Old Province of Quebec*; University of Toronto Press for *Movements of Political Protest in Canada 1640-1840* by S. D. Clark and "The Merchants of Nova Scotia and the American Revolution" by W. B. Kerr in *Canadian Historical Review*.

NOTE TO THE READER

In order to distinguish interjections made by the author in quoted works from interjections already existing in such works, the former have been placed in italics in square brackets, the latter simply in square brackets.

Introduction

A. GENERAL OBSERVATIONS

The American Revolution can be considered one of the more crucial events in Canadian history. The Revolution not only permanently shattered the vast British North American Colonial Empire, but it also profoundly affected the historical evolution of Canada. Professor A. R. M. Lower observed:

Of greater moment than the boundary settlement was the parting itself. Here surely was the profoundest depth of the Revolution. For the parting had been in bad blood. The race was broken. Neither Englishmen nor Canadians, especially Canadians, have realized to this day what Revolution really means, how wide and enduring is the gulf that it opens up between the winning and the losing sides. . . .*

For some Canadian historians the failure of the Revolution in Quebec and Nova Scotia was directly responsible for the weakness of the radical political tradition in Canada. Professor Frank Underhill lamented that:

In Canada we have no revolutionary tradition; and our historians, political scientists, and philosophers have assiduously tried to educate us to be proud of this fact. How can such a people expect their democracy to be as dynamic as the democracies of Britain and France and the United States have been?†

But for others, the Revolution meant the beginning of a distinct and unique Canadian identity based largely upon the "allegiance and the legislative supremacy of the King in Parliament."†† In Canada, therefore, as in the United States, the Revolution has meant quite different things to different people.

The refusal of both Quebec and Nova Scotia to become a

*Excerpt taken from *Colony to Nation* by Professor A. R. M. Lower. Reprinted by permission of Longmans Canada Limited.

†See especially: F. H. Underhill, *In Search of Canadian Liberalism* (Toronto: Macmillan Company of Canada, Limited, 1960), p. 12.

††W. L. Morton, *The Canadian Identity* (Toronto: University of Toronto Press, 1961), p. 100.

part of the revolutionary movement in 1775 and 1776 is of some consequence for students of American and *Canadian history. For almost a century, American scholars have been vigorously debating the actual causes of the Revolution. But almost to a man, these scholars, whether they stress economic, social or constitutional issues or the general impact of ideas, have evaded a thorough examination of the colonies that refused to join the Revolution. Such an examination is imperative if one hopes to meet, in a sophisticated manner, the challenge of what Professor Edmund S. Morgan referred to as "The American Revolution: Revisions in Need of Revising."* The perceptive comparative method provides a new approach to the perplexing problem of causation in the American Revolution.*

To many Canadians, who are desperately searching for a sense of national identity, a clear understanding of why Quebec and Nova Scotia refused to join the Revolution may help to suggest a few answers to their difficult problem. But the answers may not be especially enlightening or satisfying. Henri Bourassa may have been cutting very close to the heart of the matter when in reply to a question of why French Canadians chose not to join the Revolution he answered:

It was all very simple; we had to choose between the English of Boston and the English of London. The English of London were farther away and we hated them less.†

Why Nova Scotia and Quebec refused to join the American Revolution in 1775 and 1776 poses a fascinating historical question. It is noteworthy that so many Canadian historians have been concerned with providing a relevant answer. Perhaps Canadian historiography is not still in its infancy.

It should be kept in mind that in 1775 and 1776, the colonies of Quebec and Nova Scotia together stretched from the Mississippi River in the west, to the tip of Cape Breton Island in the east. In terms of present-day Canadian territory, the colony of Quebec covered the provinces of Ontario and Quebec and the colony of Nova Scotia included the provinces of New Brunswick and Nova

---

*E. S. Morgan, "The American Revolution: Revisions in Need of Revising," *William and Mary Quarterly*, 3rd Series, XIV (January 1957), 3-15.

†H. Neatby, "Canadianism—A Symposium," Canadian Historical Association *Report* (1956), 74.

Scotia. Quebec had a population of some 90,000, most of whom were French-speaking, while Nova Scotia had approximately 20,000 inhabitants, most of whom were New Englanders. The tiny undeveloped colony soon to be known as Prince Edward Island and the larger colony of Newfoundland were effectively protected from the revolutionary thrust from the south by their isolation and their British orientation.

Neither Nova Scotia's nor Quebec's response to the American Revolution should be looked at in complete isolation. Both colonies were on the northern periphery of the Thirteen Colonies and both reacted iin approxiimately the same manner to the early revolutionary movement. Professor W. H. Nelson has stated:

. . . All that the Tory regions, the mountain and maritime frontiers, had in common was that both suffered or were threatened with economic and political subjugation by richer adjoining areas. The geographical concentration of the Tories was in peripheral areas, regions already in decline, or not yet risen to importance. . . .

In any case, wherever regions newly or thinly settled touched the sea, there the Revolution was weakest: in Quebec, in Nova Scotia, in Georgia, and in New York where the Hudson carried the Atlantic world into the mountains. . . .*

B. THE BROAD CONTEXT

J. B. BREBNER (1945)
NORTH ATLANTIC TRIANGLE

The American Revolution should be seen as, among other things, a major readjustment of the carefully balanced forces making up what J. B. Brebner has called the "North Atlantic Triangle." Such an overview is of primary importance in order to place the events of 1775 and 1776 in Nova Scotia and Quebec, as well as the ensuing battle of interpretations, in their proper perspective. Probably the best such treatment is to be found in Brebner's North Atlantic Triangle *published in 1945.*

. . . Viewed in terms of Anglo-American relations, the exact provisions of the Quebec Act of 1774 were much less important than

---

*W. H. Nelson, *The American Tory* (Oxford: Oxford University Press, 1961), pp. 87-88.

the interpretations which embittered Americans placed upon them. In the first place, the Act, although the end product of almost ten years of systematic endeavors to work out an appropriate government for a large body of colonists of alien character, was passed in the pestilent company of the so-called Intolerable Acts, whose evident aim was to bring the older American colonies to heel. Tainted by this association, its statutory establishment of the civil law, the nonrepresentative government, the seigneurial system, and the tithe-supported Roman Catholicism to which the Canadians had been accustomed, was naturally, if uncritically, regarded as the systematic re-creation of the old northern threat to the coastal colonies, this time for British ends. In spite of the fact that the Act contained a clause which expressly provided 'that nothing herein contained relative to the boundary of the province of Quebec shall in any wise affect the boundaries of any other colony,' irritated 'old Americans' ignored this and pointed to the new boundaries of Quebec, which had been extended to include most of the Trans-Appalachian territory north of the Ohio and westward to the Mississippi and the Lake of the Woods. This was a quite defensible arrangement for the attachment of the unsettled mid-continental fur area to its natural outlet and seat of governmental regulation, but it was only too easy to argue that its real intention was to write finis to the ambitions and claims of the older colonies to expand westward beyond the mountains.

To the delegates at Philadelphia [*at the Continental Congress*], the Quebec situation presented a harsh dilemma. For generations their peoples had been damning the French for their submissive acceptance of authority in church and state, and for the barrier which they had presumed to set up along the Appalachian ridge. The Act of 1774 seemed to indicate that in these matters the victory of 1760 had brought about no change. On the other hand, however, the French had been so recently conquered that presumably they would have less love than hate for Great Britain and might the more easily be won over to the side of the Congress. It was known, too, that while the Quebec Act was highly congenial to Canadian churchmen because it restored ecclesiastical authority and legalized tithes, and to Canadian landlords because it re-established the obligations of the feudal system, it was resented by a large number of the habitants who had for fifteen years been taking some advantage of the fact that there was no law to compel them to pay dues either to priest or to seigneur. The problem, then, was how to pump up among the rebellious British colonies a convincing display of friendly fervor toward the Canadians while at the very same time the Quebec Act was being denounced as the Machiavellian work of the tyrant George III and his subservient Parliament.

The behavior of Georgia falls outside the Canadian-American relationship, but Nova Scotia provides an interesting example of how a region which was on the outskirts of the revolution was so torn by conflicting forces that it was reduced almost to passivity. By 1775 the province contained seventeen to eighteen thousand settlers, of whom at least three-quarters were New Englanders. Yet during the period of their migration and settlement since 1749, New England had been so concerned with what seemed more important matters that her long-established economic grasp on the province had gradually weakened. In Halifax, the capital, therefore, the usual colonial oligarchy of officialdom, finance, and business had fallen under the sway of a London mercantile group which had the advantage of enjoying the confidence of the colonial authorities in England. In Nova Scotia they were able to exercise a remarkably free hand because the representative system was heavily weighted to favor the propertied classes of Halifax, both locally and in terms of the whole province, and because distance and expense made it nearly impossible for the elected representatives of the impoverished out-settlements to attend the sessions of the legislature.

As the revolutionary tensions heightened, the Nova Scotians found that the sea cut off most of them from direct contact with their former homelands in New England and that roadless Nova Scotian wildernesses separated their settlements from each other. Sporadic outbursts of many sorts all over the province made it obvious where the sympathies of a majority of the people naturally lay; but it was impossible for them to get together, to maintain close relations with New England, to bend the provincial administration to their will, or to break down the private and public controls which were exercised from London. Loyalism not only had a natural appeal in pensionary Halifax, but it also promised to confer many material benefits, and Halifax was determined to keep the lid on the out-settlements in order to reap them. By a beautiful irony, the very people who had conquered Acadia, expelled the

Acadians, and occupied their lands now had forced upon them the curse which had once lain upon their victims, that is, of being caught between the millstones of a persistent North American conflict.

Newfoundland, at the outer end of the great northeastward arc of the Atlantic Coast, was so far from the center of active hostilities that there were no compulsions stringent enough to draw her into decisive positive action. The seas and shores within the great Labrador-Gaspé-Grand Banks triangle were still an international region where Newfoundlanders, English West Countrymen, Frenchmen, Iberians, Channel Islanders, Canadians, Nova Scotians, and New Englanders followed pursuits which were competitive in the main, but often complementary enough to blur the outlines of any single rending division. The fact that the New Englanders were traders in fish rather more than fishermen, for instance, meant that their rivalry with Great Britain was more one part of the great mercantile struggle between them than an urgent competition for territory.

Thus, taking British North America as a whole in 1774, the fires of imminent revolution may have been glowing fiercely in a number of places near the geographical center, but the heat grew less as it radiated outward to the margins. Generally speaking, in the region from South Carolina to southern New Hampshire the hot cores of anti-British agitation were near enough the melting point to form some kind of an amalgam, but outside that area various influences, added to distance from the center, made a larger agglomeration either very difficult or impossible. In some cases it was definitely repugnant. Georgia, Vermont, Maine, and Nova Scotia hung in the balance; East and West Florida, the West Indies, Bermuda, Newfoundland, and Hudson Bay barely felt the compulsions of the hot passions emanating from Philadelphia; and Quebec was too alien to it all to be able to respond either way with any assurance. No single formula, of course, can embrace the variegated responses of Britain's colonies in North America to attempted central control, but, if an approximation would serve, it would be found in the maturity of ten or eleven of the central continental colonies. In terms of substantial, well-rooted populations, political aptitude in libertarian English institutions, and economic resources and resourcefulness, they were grown-up enough to resent oppressive parental authority to the point of defying it.

The open revolution, which began in 1775 and turned loose such a host of clashing forces, was a curious affair in many ways. Great Britain started out with the hope that a resolute show of force would settle things without enough fighting to create abiding hatreds. In the more independent colonies an angry minority refused thus to be impressed, and by resolute, skilful attacks on officials, soldiers, and sailors, gradually goaded the shaky federal Congress and the hesitant British leviathan into a fight to a finish. Then it became clear, on the one hand, that Great Britain lacked the ability to create and maintain a force sufficient to conquer her colonists and their vast domains, while on the other, the Congress could not win enough support in the colonies to do more than wage a fairly useful brand of guerrilla warfare.

In this revolution, therefore, a conclusion had either to await exhaustion or be hastened by the stimulus and response of outside intervention. Great Britain bought German troops outright. The United Colonies were more fortunate because France and Spain were thirsting for revenge and saw a chance to fish profitably in troubled waters by allying themselves with the rebels. Holland also formally ranged herself on the American side and much of the rest of Europe showed similar sympathies. Meanwhile, at Westminster and throughout England, resentment against the effects of George III's interference in politics made his critics think of him somewhat as the Americans did and persuaded many of them to applaud and help the revolutionary cause at home and abroad. Elsewhere in Europe the intellectual distinction of the rebel leaders and the artistry of their propaganda made a deep appeal to those liberals who despaired of ever rousing European societies to redemption from conservatism and decay. Not only soldiers of fortune, but idealists from the British Isles, France, Germany, and central Europe crossed the Atlantic to provide material and moral support for the American War of Independence.

The war itself was largely fought along classic, predictable lines. Before it broke out in earnest Ethan Allen and his Vermonters made a quick dash at Ticonderoga and the Champlain-Richelieu Valley, and New England privateers tried to brush aside the British barriers to the Bay of Fundy and Nova Scotia. After these preliminary skirmishes, Washington and the Congress settled down to the modification of the traditional plan of campaign for North America which was forced upon them by their lack of a navy. Without one, Nova Scotia could not be conquered unless Nova Scotians did the job, and even then they could not consolidate their province with New England. A few Nova Scotians made the effort in spite of Washington's warnings, and failed as he saw they would fail. The mass of the population, most of them only fifteen years or less away from New England, could only fall back upon neutrality—the very device which the Acadians had clung to during the Anglo-French wars. The 'neutral French,' as the Acadians had been called by the British colonials, were thus succeeded by the 'neutral Yankees' in Nova Scotia.

The same lack of a navy made an attack on Quebec by sea impossible and its retention, if captured by land, unlikely. Nevertheless, Benedict Arnold was willing to chance it by leading a small army overland through the empty wilderness by the Kennebec River to the height of land and thence down the Chaudière River to face the grim old fortress across the St. Lawrence. This astonishing gamble had its justification only if two other gambles succeeded. Preliminary missions from the Congress to the American element in Montreal had on the whole been discouragingly received, but a minority there, angry over Carleton's attitude toward them and the apparent termination by the recent Quebec Act of their hopes for "the rights of Englishmen," showed some willingness to cooperate. In addition, the Congress had addressed an ingenious, if naïve, letter of appeal to the French Canadians to throw off the British yoke, and this was creating some disturbing ferments among the independent habitants as it worked upon their uneasiness over the authoritarian implications of the Quebec Act. These favoring circumstances could presumably be enlarged by prompt use of American military force against the western part of Quebec in order to create a base in the interior, north of New York and New England. Then an American army which had followed the Lake Champlain route to Montreal from the Hudson could advance down the St. Lawrence to join Arnold for the capture of Quebec, and the combined forces, if they could buy or otherwise win some popular support, might make it even harder for Great Britain to reconquer the province of Quebec from the sea than it would be, for instance, to conquer Pennsylvania.

This daring plan failed. Early in November, Montreal fell easily to an overwhelming Hudson army under Montgomery because there were less than eight hundred British troops in the whole province and the Canadians would not defend the region, but Governor Carleton managed to escape down river to Quebec. Here he was suddenly confronted by Arnold and the tattered seven hundred who had struggled across the wilderness and arrived with little more equipment than what they could carry on their backs. Montgomery, hearing of their arrival, left his snug winter quarters and went down the river to support Arnold. Most of his troops had gone home, so that after he had manned garrisons he had only about three hundred Americans and the moderate amount of support in services of supply and transport which his cause and his hard cash obtained from the Canadian people. On New Year's Eve, 1775, he and Arnold daringly risked an attack on Carleton's improvised garrison and attenuated defenses. But Montgomery was killed, Arnold was wounded, siege artillery was lacking, and Quebec's walls were more stable than Jericho's. More than half of the American force was killed, or captured. In May the British fleet arrived at Quebec with a large expeditionary force, whereas the Congress had been reduced to sending to its reinforced, but smallpox-ridden and ill-equipped armies mere paper promises instead of bullion with which to pay the Canadians for supplies and services. The Americans, their hazard thrown and lost, retreated up the St. Lawrence and Richelieu to Ticonderoga again, taking with them a few French Canadians and some Montreal merchants whose assistance to the invaders had made Quebec too hot to hold them.*

In accounting for Nova Scotia's and Quebec's failure in 1775 and 1776 to join the Revolution, Brebner accurately singled out the importance of British seapower. But like so many historians who had written before him and others who would follow him, Brebner tended to interpret events in the light of what he knew would eventually happen rather than to view them through the eyes of the men of the time. Hindsight, of course, is extremely useful for the historian and the student, but it is imperative that the historical problem be examined, not only from "above and beyond," but also from the point of view of the people concerned.

---

*J. B. Brebner, *North Atlantic Triangle* (New York: Columbia University Press, 1958), pp. 49-55.

PART ONE

Why did Nova Scotia refuse to join the American Revolution in 1775-76?

INTRODUCTION

Throughout the period of the American Revolution, Nova Scotia was little more than a political expression for a number of widely scattered and isolated communities. These stretched from Pictou on Northumberland Strait to Canso, from Canso to Halifax, from the colony's capital to Maugerville on the St. John River, and to the tiny outpost of Passamaquoddy on the St. Croix. At the end of the Seven Years' War many land-hungry settlers from Rhode Island, New Hampshire, Massachusetts and Connecticut had pushed up into the fertile regions bordering the Bay of Fundy. This area had been abandoned in 1755 by the Acadians when they were expelled from the peninsula.

In 1775 Nova Scotia had a population of approximately only 20,000 inhabitants, three-quarters of whom were New Englanders with strong economic, cultural and family ties with their former homeland. Because Nova Scotia was virtually New England's northeastern frontier and was peopled by a majority of recently-arrived New Englanders, one would have expected the colony, in 1775 and 1776, to have joined the other New England colonies in their successful attempt to shatter the framework of the British colonial system. But instead, Nova Scotia remained loyal to the British Crown.*

A. CONTEMPORARY OPINION

There were three main groups in Nova Scotia during "The Critical Years, 1775-76," each of which had a different attitude towards the "American Revolution." A small but vociferous minority, residing

* W. B. Kerr, "Nova Scotia in the Critical Years, 1775-6," *Dalhousie Review* (April 1932), 97.

in the western section of the colony, enthusiastically supported the rebels. A second group, not very large but British to the core, and concentrated in Halifax, favoured the existing colonial relationship. The third, undoubtedly the most numerous, made up largely of New Englanders living east of the Chignecto Isthmus, endeavoured to pursue a policy of neutrality. It is interesting to note that this policy was precisely the same as that condemned by many New Englanders when it was adopted by the Acadians two decades earlier.

i Pro-Revolution

1 ANONYMOUS LETTER TO GENERAL WASHINGTON (1776)

On February 8, 1776 an anonymous inhabitant of the Chignecto Isthmus region wrote to General Washington and declared that "The generality of the Province . . . sympathize with the Colonies."

Sir: You may reasonably imagine that it is presumptuous in me to take such liberty in writing to your Excellency; still, its going from one whose principles are actuated from the genuine feelings of liberty, and an indelible anxiety for the happiness of his country, animates an assurance that it will meet rather with a feeling of sympathy than censure; more particularly as it is addressed to you, sir, who is at the head of that Army which is opposing the mandates of a corrupt and despotick Ministry, whose views and intent can be founded upon no other principles than to bring the subjects of *Britain* to as abject slavery as the subjects of the most arbitrary Eastern monarchy. Sensible I am of the importance of this proceeding, my inability of performing anything in this great struggle, and the danger I expose myself and family to in being treated with that accumulated vengeance used by such men, who are actuated by publick, as well as private prejudices; still, my fear and dread is yet more when I consider the state of my country, that, by lying passive, I expose myself and posterity to be bound in chains of slavery and wretchedness, and not only that, but have that infamous epithet entailed upon them, of being like those sluggish and slothful wretches, as represented of the tribes of *Issachar*. You will, therefore, pardon this impudence of mine.

The great contest between *Britain* and *America* has hitherto been only treated with speculation amongst us. A spirit of sympathy, I presume, for our brethren on the Continent, reigns in the breasts of the generality of the inhabitants. With gladness and cheerfulness would we be active in the glorious struggle, had our situation and circumstances been any way such that there was the least glimpse of success; but our remoteness from the other Colonies, and our form of Government, joined with the indigent circumstances of the inhabitants, render it in a manner impossible, without succour from some other quarter.

Time not permitting, and my mind impressed with accumulated troubles for our situation, nor is it necessary, for the present intention, to give a detail of the different proceedings and managements of Government; so much will suffice, to give your Excellency an idea of the rise of our impending calamity, if Providence does not stir up some means to prevent it.

The generality of the Province, as I before mentioned, sympathize with the Colonies. The least encouragement or opportunity would have excited the people to join in the defence of the liberty of *America*, always rejoicing when they heard any flying report that an invasion was intended. A necessity there was that the rulers in Government should use every means and method to prevent giving uneasiness to the people, if they had a mind to preserve peace. Yet, notwithstanding, the men at the head of the Government, with their emissaries, following the example of their patrons, the Ministry, stimulated with an expectation of recommending themselves by showing their zealousness for the prerogative, prompts on the Governour to some proclamations laying certain restraints on the people. Then, joining in associations, offering their lives and fortunes in the defence of the supremacy of the Parliament; and then, to complete the matter, advise the Governour to call the Assembly together at a time when the small-pox was raging at a great degree. Many of the country members could not attend on account of the distemper. A bill was passed for raising a regiment by ballot; and another for raising a tax to support them. The preamble to the latter was such, that, in my view, it carried the greatest implication of a declaration of war against the Colonies. This flagrant proof of the intention of these miscreants roused a spirit among the people, and publick declarations were made which before were not heard. Some were immediately for applying to your Excellency. Business was entirely stagnated. Nothing to be heard but war—this Country in particular. The inhabitants being called to appear by the Commanding Officer of

Militia, they complied with the order; and, when met, they all, to a man, charged the officers, on their peril, to draw a person. The inhabitants then agreed that an Address, Remonstrance, and Petition, be sent to the Governour, praying his suspending the execution of said acts, and to dissolve the House of Assembly, and call a new one to meet immediately. The Governour gave no other answer than ordering the officers of Militia and tax-gatherers to desist, for the present, the putting the acts into execution. On the receipt of this, the County of *Cumberland* again met, and resolved, almost unanimously, that it was no way satisfactory, and that it was only to delay time till a number of troops could be distributed through the different parts, as we had sufficient reason to imagine so by the preparation and other intelligences at *Halifax*. We have, therefore, again petitioned, pressing his Excellency the Governour to answer our former request, by dissolving the Assembly, and, for the first time, hinting to him our feeling for the commotions in the *British Empire*, etc. In this time some recruiting parties came among us, as also a person whom we have found to be a spy. These, with others who live among us whose principles are actuated by private prejudices, besides their enthusiasm for arbitrary authority, are making strong solicitations to have troops sent among us, the fear of which has occasioned much disorder and discontent among us. Many are afraid of speaking. There are, also, among us several families which lately came from *England*. They, in general, speak something in favour of Parliament, and are willing to submit to little taxes, as they have been accustomed to pay such heavy ones in their own country. These encourage the minions of Government. We can have no certainty how matters are passing. News is constantly propagated to the disadvantage of the *Americans*, and of the intentions and success of the other side, and that almost every foreign power intends assisting *Britain*. Sometimes we have a flying report that the *Americans* have allies to help them; but this is generally stifled. All these things keep us in a flutter. The straggling manner in which people have settled this new country makes it very difficult, and, in a manner, almost impossible for them to act either offensively or defensively. The people, in general, have great families, which will occasion a lamentable scene should *British* Troops arrive here before any succour comes from your Excellency. We would greatly rejoice could we be able to join with the other Colonies; but we must have other assistance before we can act publickly. I would observe to your Excellency, concerning the *Acadians*, I have dwelt among them near six-and-twenty years. I am well acquainted with their manners and ways. I have taken great pains in conversing with them concerning their commotions. They are, to a man, wholly inclined to the cause of *America*. I have often pitied them in their situation, and the manner of proceedings against them from time to time. I have made proposals to them, and promised, if ever in my power, to do my utmost for their relief, and to lay the state of their matter before the honourable the Continental Congress, not doubting but they would be relieved. By this opportunity, I have sent a young man belonging to themselves; he may be able to answer any questions your Excellency may want to know.

A Committee was chosen lately by the inhabitants to fall upon such methods as might be thought conducive for the publick safety. On their meeting two or three times, suspicion arose that they intended sending to the Continent; the news of which was sent immediately to *Halifax*. The Committee, perceiving these things, found they could not continue, as they subjected themselves to be made prisoners. They therefore agreed to lay aside the sending to *New England* as a Committee; but if any should choose to do anything of themselves, they might. The bearer, Captain *Jonathan Eddy*, declared that he would immediately set off by land, and lay our situation before your Excellency. A number drew up a small incorrect address, to recommend him to your Excellency. He will, no doubt, fully prove that he is capable for the undertaking. I have also, at the same time, sent two *Frenchmen*, to return immediately from Machias, in order to know what we are to expect.

Your Excellency may see by this, with the other information you may receive, our situation. You have, no doubt, an unlimited power to help the distressed in this critical time. I trust and rely that this, joined with your own humane disposition, will excite your Excellency to give us assistance. Should your Excellency incline helping us, it would be necessary to take care how any troops come. My grand view in this is, to prevent the effusion of blood; for should it be known when they come, I imagine that a force would be sent to oppose. The present situation of the Province respecting force is very trifling; and the fear our great men are in concerning an invasion makes it more so. They have but about two hundred regular troops in *Halifax*, including a number of raw recruits from *Newfoundland* and other places. The Twenty-Seventh Regiment, lately arrived, is stationed in the naval yard, and there endeavouring to fortify round the town; but I think it is but trifling. We have this comfort, that, should no other troops arrive, they may not send up to molest us. Had we, at this present time, two or three hundred men, it would secure all that part of the Province between this and *Halifax,* and am convinced that that number would prevent five thousand from coming through the woods. Captain *Eddy* will make known to your Excellency the most suitable manner how to introduce troops. I am, it may be said, more particular in this, in order to serve some friends. One of my brothers is an officer in the regiment at *Halifax*. Galling as this is to me, and the feeling of anguish for this calamity, will nowise deter me in my pursuit for the welfare of the publick. Determined I am to prosecute the matter, if *God* should spare me, to establish those rights and privileges in this Province which should, by right, be enjoyed by every human being. But should your Excellency, with the honourable the Continental Congress, determine not to give any assistance, it must occasion the most direful and horrible consequences. Let me beseech your Excellency to help us. Give us an opportunity of joining with the other Colonies. It all depends upon your bounty.

I must once more plead for your forgiveness for this liberty I have taken, as, also, excuse the incorrectness of my writing. I have not time to copy. And further, must earnestly request your keeping this from the publick. Much other information could be given; but the hurry of the departure of the bearer prevents my saying more. I refer to him. Any assistance I can give your Excellency, either by intelligence or otherwise, I shall esteem it an honour and duty to perform.

My best wishes for the success of your arms. May the Supreme Ruler of the Universe protect you. May the civil and religious liberties of *America* stand firm and unshaken to the latest posterity, is my earnest prayer.

I am, with profound respect, your Excellency's most devoted, most obedient, and very humble servant.

To His Excellency *George Washington.**

---

* P. Force, *American Archives,* Fourth Series (Washington, 1844), V, pp. 936-938.

2 RESOLUTIONS OF THE INHABITANTS OF THE MAUGERVILLE AREA (1776)

In May of 1776 the inhabitants of the Maugerville area showed that they had become a part of the revolutionary movement by agreeing to the following resolutions:

1stly Resolved. That we can see no shadow of Justice in that Extensive Claim of the British Parliment (viz) the Right to Enacting Laws binding on the Colonies in all Cases whatsoever. This System if once Established (we Conceive) hath a Direct tendency to Sap the foundation, not only of Liberty that Dearest of names, but of property that best of subjects.
2ndly Resolved. That as tyrany ought to be Resisted in its first appearance we are Convinced that the united Provinces are just in their proceeding in this Regard.
3rdly Resolved. That it is our Minds and Desire to submit ourselves to the government of the Massachusetts Bay and that we are Ready with our Lives and fortunes to Share with them the Event of the present Struggle for Liberty, however God in his Providence may order it.
4ly Resolved. That a Committee be Chosen to Consist of twelve Men who shall Immediately make application to the Massachusetts Congress or general assembly for Relief, at that S[ai]d Committee or Major part of them shall Conduct all Matter Civill or Military in this Country till further Regulations be made.
5ly Resolved. That we and Each of us will most strictly adhere to all such measures as our S[ai]d Committee or the Major Part of them shall from time to time prescribe for our Conduct and that we will support and Defend them in this Matter at the Expence of our Lives and fortunes if Called thereto.
6ly Resolved. That we will Immediately put ourselves in the best posture of Defence in our power, that to this End we will prevent all unnecessary use of gun Powder or other ammunition in our Custody.
7ly Resolved. That if any of us shall hereafter, Know of any person or persons that shall by any ways or means Endeavour to prevent or Counteract this our Design, we will Immediately give notice thereof to the Committee that proper Measures may be taken for our Safety.

8ly Resolved. . . . we will share in and submit to the Event of this undertaking however it may terminate, to the true performance of all which we bind and obligate ourselves firmly each to other on penalty of being Esteemed Enemies and traitors to our Country and Submitting ourselves to popular Resentment.*

Some months later the Maugerville inhabitants were still "Almost universally to be hearty in the Cause."† Twenty-seven settlers joined Jonathan Eddy's "liberating army" from Machias in its unsuccessful attempt to drive the British from Fort Cumberland on the Chignecto Isthmus. Eddy's rash attempt to capture Fort Cumberland failed not only because he lacked artillery, but also because his men were poorly trained, undisciplined and badly led. Even though the Eddy Rebellion, by any broad strategic standards, was quite insignificant in the larger revolutionary context, it is of some importance as representing a road Nova Scotia could have *followed .Maugerville's choice, however, was not to be Nova Scotia's destiny.*††

ii Anti-Revolution

3 LETTER TO THE NOVA SCOTIA GAZETTE AND THE WEEKLY CHRONICLE (1776)

On September 10, 1776 there appeared the following sharply-worded letter to the editor:

. . . The Demagogues, which raised this disturbance, are a motely crew of hungry lawyers, men of broken fortunes, young persons eager to push themselves in the world, others, gentlemen of opulence, vain & blustering—Amongst this medley there are several of good party, and great reading, but withal little versed in the complicated interests, and springs, which move the great political world, because untutored in the Courts of Europe, where alone that science is to be acquired—These could not miss perceiving the

---

* F. Kidder, *Military Operations in Eastern Maine and Nova Scotia During the Revolution* (Albany: J. Munsell, 1867), pp. 64-65.

† Quoted in D. C. Harvey, "Machias and the Invasion of Nova Scotia," Canadian Historical Association *Report* (1932), 21

†† See George A. Rawlyk, "The American Revolution and Nova Scotia Reconsidered," *Dalhousie Review*, Vol. 43, No. 3, 1963, 387-390.

growing importance, as they call it, of America, and what she might one day arrive to: so far indeed they judged with propriety, if they would only give time, and leave her to herself; but the greatness of the object dazzled the eyes of their understanding; and they began to think Empire, without considering the infant state of their country, how much it is [*in*] want of every requisite for war, what a mighty nation they have to contend with, & that the united interest of every other nation in Europe likewise forbids their being anything more than dependent colonies—However, as if envying their prosperity, they hastened to bring on the great and glorious day, which would hail them masters of a quarter of the globe; and set up claims which, they thought, would either place them in that elevated station or in one more suitable to their present condition viz. to make the Mother Country drudge and slave to support, and protect them, for yet a while longer, without contributing a farthing more towards that expence that they should think proper; afterwards how soon they could no longer bear the thoughts of dependence, and that they could emancipate themselves (which indeed this mode would soon enable them to do) to dispute the expediency of the purposes for which their aids were to be applied, offer only a triffling sum, taking that opportunity of declaring for independence and maintain it too. . . .

The menaces of the Americans to run to arms, their violent proceedings in the first stage of the insurrection, their levying troops, which every where belongs to the executive branch, so notoriously . . . their collecting warlike weapons . . . were all such strong acts of rebellion as no government could put up with, it destroyed the merits of their cause, were it otherwise good: for resisting legal authority in that manner, however warrantable when oppression is intollerable, is yet a nice affair, and can only be justified, when tyranny is well ascertained, generally felt, and after the milder methods of redress have been ineffectually tried; which the impartial world is satisfied was by no means their case. . . .

Had they acted in a moderate, dutiful, and justifiable manner, like subjects averse to break with their Sovereign, like men, who even in their own cause wished only for material justice, and not actuated by any indirect views but by the force of the principles, they protested; there is no doubt but whatever appeared to them harsh and dangerous, in the claims of Great Britain, would have been departed from, and matters settled on the basis of indulgence to the Colonies, and justice to the Mother country. But his Majesty's Paternal voice was bar'd access to his beloved subject; He could not treat with them, but thro' the false, and villainous medium of the proud demonogues, who paid no regard to truth, to loyalty, to peace or justice.*

4 LIEUTENANT-GOVERNOR ARBUTHNOT'S OBSERVATIONS (1776)

The Nova Scotia Gazette, *printed in Halifax, consistently reflected the opinions of "the substantial people"† of the Colony. Lieutenant-Governor Mariot Arbuthnot observed on December 31, 1776:*

the truth is My Lord the wealthy people in general are loyal, the sectaries are not so, nor never will until their clergy are under some control . . . the New England people and Acadians . . . are bitter bad subjects.††

Arbuthnot, like most supporters of the British, was unwilling to distinguish between those New Englanders in Nova Scotia who had chosen to walk the knife-edge of neutrality and a relatively small number that had already moved into the "rebel" camp.

iii Neutrality

5 PETITIONS OF NEW ENGLANDERS IN NOVA SCOTIA (1775)

Ground between the millstones of contending loyalties, most New Englanders in Nova Scotia decided to adopt a neutral posture. Their point of view can best be seen in two petitions—the first from the Yarmouth area and the second from the Amherst-Sackville region.

We do all of us profess to be true Friends & Loyal Subjects to George our King. We were almost all of us born in New England, we have Fathers, Brothers & Sisters in that Country, divided betwixt natural affection to our nearest relations, and good Faith and

---

* *Nova Scotia Gazette and the Weekly Chronicle*, September 10, 1776. Modern spelling has been used to clarify the meaning of the letter.

† *Public Archives of Nova Scotia (P.A.N.S.)*, Vol. 45, Arbuthnot to Lord George Germain, April 26, 1776.

†† *Ibid.*, Arbuthnot to Germain, December 31, 1776.

Friendship to our King and Country, we want to know, if we may be permitted at this time to live in a peaceable State, as we look on that to be the only situation in which we with our Wives and Children, can be in any tolerable degree safe.*

The dispute arising between Great Britain and her Colonies has no way reached this quarter nor can we find any grounds of complaint wherein any act of violence have been committed . . . nor are we any ways apprehensive of any danger . . . except this Militia Bill is enforced. Those of us who belong to New England, being invited into the Province by Governor Lawrence's Proclamation it must be the greatest piece of cruelty and imposition for them to be subjected to march into different parts in Arms against their friends and relations. Still should any person or persons presume to molest us in our present situation, we are always ready to defend ourselves and property.†

The Nova Scotia New Englanders were certainly not willing to fight against their "nearest relations" nor were they eager to participate actively in the revolutionary cause. They first wanted to be certain in which direction the bandwagon was rolling before they jumped on it. Until that time they were content to remain neutral even though their sympathies probably lay with the rebels. Practical and strategic considerations, however, effectively countered their sympathies.

B. NINETEENTH AND TWENTIETH CENTURY VIEWS

1 BEAMISH MURDOCH (1866)
INTENSE LOYALTY AND AFFECTION

At least one Nineteenth Century Nova Scotian historian, Beamish Murdoch of Halifax, attempted in 1866 to explain Nova Scotia's refusal to join the Revolution. He admitted that in 1775 and 1776 "the prospects of Nova Scotia were . . . especially gloomy."†† *But he argued that the New England Nova Scotians were not in any was sympathetic to the revolutionary cause.*

---

* Quoted in J. B. Brebner, *The Neutral Yankees of Nova Scotia* (New York: Columbia University Press, 1937), p. 291.

† *P.A.N.S.*, Vol. 364, The inhabitants of Cumberland to Governor Legge, December 23, 1775.

†† B. Murdoch, *A History of Nova Scotia or Acadie* (Halifax: J. Barnes, 1866), II, p. 562.

None of the settlers of the province were under so great personal obligation to the Crown as the farmers from New England, to whom the French lands had been made a gift; and when they came to Nova Scotia they were full of intense loyalty and affection to the British government, and were not mixed up with the troubles and discords that subsequently affected New England.*

Murdoch's assessment of the mood of Nova Scotians in 1775 and 1776 probably tells us more about Nova Scotia during the 1860's when his history was written than it does about the colony during the early revolutionary years. Murdoch, like most leading Nova Scotians, was as British as the British, if not more so. Consequently, he felt compelled to use his History of Nova Scotia *to prove that true Nova Scotians had always been "eminently loyal."*

2 EMILY P. WEAVER (1904)
LACK OF DISCONTENT AND LEADERSHIP, PLUS HALIFAX INTERESTS

It was not until 1904 that a serious historical journal carried an article dealing with Nova Scotia's attitude towards the Revolution. Emily P. Weaver's "Nova Scotia and New England During the Revolution" raised the vitally important question of why Nova Scotia "continue[d] loyal to the crown of England."† Weaver may have asked the right question but she did everything in her power to evade answering it in a straightforward manner. She rightly questioned the validity of Murdoch's thesis by observing that

. . . it is difficult to understand why Nova Scotia did not follow the lead of New England. The charactor of the population did not promise any high degree of loyalty. It was composed largely of emigrants from New England, who had only recently, at the time of the Stamp Act agitation, left their old homes; and there was another element of danger to the British connection in the presence of a number of Acadians who had escaped the intended doom of exile or had contrived to return to the province. . . . The hostility of the Acadians usually involved that of the Indians, who were still much under French influence.††

---

* *Ibid.*, p. 570.
† E. P. Weaver, "Nova Scotia and New England during the Revolution," *American Historical Review*, X (October 1904), 52.
††*Ibid.*

Weaver implied that Nova Scotia remained loyal despite the presence of the New Englanders and Acadians for three main reasons. Unfortunately, these reasons were neither developed in a satisfactory way nor were they presented in a clearcut fashion. Rather, they were buried in much superfluous prose. The first reason given was that since Nova Scotia had "practically no manufacturing. . . there was little reason for popular discontent with the navigation laws." Secondly, "the disaffected of Nova Scotia seem to have had no leader of any great power or influence,"† and the isolation of the various settlements made effective united action virtually impossible. Thirdly, Weaver maintained that:*

The interests of Halifax itself were indeed all on the side of the established order of things. Then as now it was the chief seaport, the seat of government for the province, and a British naval and military station, and in those days its prosperity, its importance, its very existence, depended on these conditions. Such specie as circulated was introduced into the country by the army and navy.††

Despite Weaver's superficial analysis of these three reasons, her pioneering study prepared the way for much more detailed and sophisticated explanations.

3 VIOLA F. BARNES (1931)

HALIFAX MERCHANTS AND GOVERNOR FRANCIS LEGGE

In 1931 Professor Viola Barnes began a decade of stimulating debate concerning the problem of Nova Scotia's response to the Revolution. It was her contention that the Halifax merchants and Governor Francis Legge were responsible for keeping Nova Scotia loyal to the Crown.

This same month of September, 1774, while Nova Scotia was experiencing the first stages of disaffection, the twelve colonies to the south (except Georgia) were in the last stages of organized protest against England's latest provocation, the Coercive Acts of 1774, directed chiefly against Massachusetts and Boston. They met in a Continental Congress and formed the Association to enforce a commercial boycott against the mother country. The sign-

---

* *Ibid.*, 56
† *Ibid.*, 57.
††*Ibid.*

ers agreed not to import anything from Great Britain or Ireland or any staples from the British West Indies; and after September 1, 1775, to export nothing thither. Any colony refusing to join was to be excluded from trade with the rest. Addresses to the colonies not represented in this Congress—Canada, St. John's, Nova Scotia, Georgia, and East and West Florida—were drawn up and dispatched with copies of the Association and other congressional papers.

The merchants of Nova Scotia saw in the impending boycott of West India trade a golden opportunity to escape from the economic bondage to New England under which the Province had suffered since the French and Indian War. A report in 1764 shows that of Nova Scotia's total exports, valued at £64,790, fish and furs worth £17,000 were disposed of through New England. The rich farm lands around the Bay of Fundy produced quantities of grain, which was marketed chiefly through Boston, because it was easier to sell to New England vessels than to ship to Halifax. This dependence on New England carriers was partly due to poor land transportation and partly to lack of local shipping. The uneven distribution of food supply left parts of Nova Scotia dependent on the outside world for provisions, and New England traders became the middlemen. They brought to Nova Scotia provisions, British manufactures, West India products, which they exchanged for fish, lumber, horses, furs, and even a small amount of hard money. There was little or no direct trade between England and Nova Scotia, because the Province had no medium of exchange and lacked sufficient specie to pay for British goods directly. Nova Scotians were, for the most part, either farmers or fishermen, but the distilleries were becoming important, thanks to the impost of 5d. a gallon on imported rum. Although it protected the local distillers, this impost bore down on general trade, because it restricted the purchase of West India rum and thus reduced the amount of products from Nova Scotia which could be sold in the islands by way of exchange. The rivalry with New England and the selfishness of local distillers, thus limited the economic outlook of Nova Scotia.

Suddenly the whole horizon of her economics opened up. If the twelve rebellious colonies chose to cut themselves off from trade with Nova Scotia and the West Indies, perhaps Nova Scotia could control her own fisheries monopolistically and appropriate

Scotia could control her own fisheries monopolistically and appropriate the West India trade.' After the various acts by the British government to restrain New England trade says Miss Barnes, 'Nova Scotia's hope of economic ascendancy, together with the financial and military support she received from the mother country, more than balanced the obligations demanded of her. . . . Nova Scotia remained loyal because the merchant class in control believed that the province profited more than it lost by the connection with the mother country, and because the governor with their help was able to prevent the radicals from stirring the people to revolt.'

Such is Miss Barnes's view, ably set forth and explained. But in assuming that events depended on the merchant class, this theory admits as the author of this article believes, a serious error. Reluctance of merchants to join the agitations was no feature peculiar to Nova Scotia. It was marked in New Hampshire and Georgia as well; and when the crisis came it was evident even in the more revolutionary colonies. This merchant, says Mr. Schlesinger, speaking of the New Englanders of 1774-5, could not see 'any commercial advantage which might accrue from pursuing the will o' the wisp of the radicals. The uncertain prospect which the radical plans held forth was not comparable with the tangible benefits which came from membership in the British Empire under existing conditions. . . . When all was said and done, the merchants knew their welfare depended upon their connection with Great Britain—upon the protection afforded by the British navy, upon the acquisition of new markets by British arms, upon legislation which fostered their shipping, subsidised certain industries and protected the merchants from foreign competition in British markets. . . . Thus there became a strong drift on the part of the colonial mercantile class to the British viewpoint of the questions at issue.' The position of the merchants was at the bottom much the same from Halifax to Savannah. But in thirteen colonies the radicals overbore both merchants and economic interests; in one they did not. The decisive factor was not the attitude of the merchants but that of the urban populace and farmers. Hence in Nova Scotia also the decisive factor was the apparently loyal attitude of populace and farmers.

In the second place it is doubtful that even the merchants of Nova Scotia were influenced by economic motives to the extent assumed by Miss Barnes. She believes that they resented their 'economic bondage' to New England, such bondage consisting in the near-monopoly of Nova Scotian carrying trade by New Englanders. But the Nova Scotians were New Englanders themselves, with nothing to prevent them from doing that carrying trade if they so desired. If they allowed their New England brothers and cousins to do it for them, they must have been satisfied with the situation. The writer has failed to find in the Nova Scotia documents any trace of hostility to New Englanders over the carrying trade or any other economic matter. As for desire to capture West Indian trade from the New Englanders, we may recall that Nova Scotia merchants had shown themselves singularly indifferent to similar opportunities in 1768-1770. Further, such capture would have been of no more than very temporary benefit, of less benefit than the loss caused by the continental boycott, unless the thirteen colonies were to become actually independent. One has serious doubts that anyone in Nova Scotia in 1774 really believed that the thirteen colonies would achieve complete independence. The general expectation was that, in the long run, some arrangement would be reached between the mother country and the colonies, in which case any Nova Scotian hopes of monopolizing fisheries and West Indian trade would die a sudden death. Further, even if a few merchants of Halifax thought of gambling on so uncertain a prospect, why did they alone yield to the temptation of making money out of Boston's predicament, they and not the men of Salem, of Marblehead, of Portsmouth, of New Haven, of southern colonies much better situated to do business with the West Indian Islands? Is it seriously contended that any New England town in 1774 would have deserted Boston in order to supplant that city in the West Indian trade? But if not, another factor beside the purely economic must have been at work in New England proper and not in Nova Scotia, the factor of common sympathy, the feeling of nationality. The absence of national feeling, then, was the decisive factor in the Nova Scotia situation rather than the presence of doubtful economic opportunities.

From every point of view it appears that Nova Scotia's New Englanders remained cold and impervious to the feeling of nationality which was impelling the thirteen colonies to try the difficult ways of revolution in those critical years. Hence, in June of 1775, the month of Bunker Hill, the assembly of Nova Scotia, composed in majority of New Englanders, and at that time at odds with Governor Legge, drew up an address to the king acknowledging in express terms 'The King in Parliament to be supreme Legislature of this province and it is our indispensable duty to pay a due proportion of the expense of this great Empire.' Hence Nova Scotia remained in perfect peace through the summer of 1775 while Legge had at his disposal only thirty-six soldiers to keep order among a population of 20,000, three quarters of whom were New Englanders. Hence, too, every attempt to raise Nova Scotia failed. Succeeding years merely confirmed the province in its stand until the Continental Congress in 1781, when drawing up a constitution for the new confederation, made provision for the admission of Canada but gave Nova Scotia up as hopeless.*

Without question, Kerr effectively demolished the "Halifax-Merchant" interpretation and also showed how ineffective Governor Legge actually was in Nova Scotia. It is clear that the influence of the Halifax merchants was largely confined to the Bedford Basin area. Their economic ties with Great Britain were admittedly strong, but they were certainly in no position to impose their will upon the rest of the colony. Most Nova Scotians reacted violently to the Halifax merchant clique that was arrogantly attempting to manipulate the economic and political life of the colony.

It appears that Kerr has underestimated the general significance of the widespread sympathy for revolutionary principles throughout most parts of Nova Scotia in 1775 and 1776. He has also failed to explain how he measured "national sentiment" or "nationalism." He mistakes the neutrality of most Nova Scotians for "tepid loyalty."† Moreover, Kerr did not place sufficient emphasis on British naval power and the isolation of most of the Nova Scotian settlements as important factors weakening the indigenous revolutionary movement.

5 D. C. HARVEY (1932-33)

THE BRITISH NAVY AND BRITISH COLONIAL POLICY

For D. C. Harvey, the superiority of the British Navy as well as British Colonial policy were largely responsible for keeping Nova Scotia in British hands in 1775 and 1776. Harvey argued that the

* Kerr, "The Merchants of Nova Scotia and the American Revolution," 33-36.
† Kerr, "Nova Scotia in the Critical Years, 1775-6," 107.

shrewd Nova Scotians "were inclined to submit to the will of the stronger." And since British naval power was infinitely superior to that of the rebels in 1775 and 1776 there was only one possible choice for the Nova Scotians to make. However, had the French come to the assistance of the American revolutionaries in 1775 rather than in 1778, the general reaction in Nova Scotia might have been radically different.*†

Harvey next dealt with the struggle for the New England form of township government in Nova Scotia. Basically the issue was whether the New Englanders who had settled in Nova Scotia after the expulsion of the Acadians would be permitted the same broad latitude in choosing local officials as they had enjoyed in New England. Eventually the struggle was resolved in favour of the Halifax government.

In principle, the Act (An Act for the Choice of Town Officers and regulating of Township, 1765) was more conservative than either the Act of 1759 or that of 1761. They had left the choice of the officers mentioned exclusively to the Grand Jury; but by the Act of 1765 the Grand Jury could only nominate two or more persons for each office; and then, out of these, the Court of Quarter Sessions (appointed by the Halifax authorities) was to *choose* and *appoint*. . . .

This Act was a complete repudiation of the New England form of Township government; and it no doubt had some influence upon the attitude of the rural townships towards the American Revolution. Certainly, some of the settlers left the Province because of their dissatisfaction with what they regarded as broken pledges. But it prevented the formation of some 20 little republics in Western Nova Scotia, and it enabled the central government both to establish communication with the Townships and to retain a check upon their activities.††

There are a number of important implications in Harvey's argument. Firstly, at least a few potential revolutionary leaders were driven out of the colony in the 1760's because of the virtual destruction of the "New England form of Township government." Secondly, the Halifax government authorities were able not only to

*Harvey, "Machias and the Invasion of Nova Scotia," 17.
† *Ibid.*, 27.
††D. C. Harvey, "The Struggle for the New England Form of Township Government in Nova Scotia," Canadian Historical Association *Report* (1933), 22.

check democratic tendencies in the New England areas of Nova Scotia but also to limit drastically the local autonomy of these areas. But can it not also be argued, using Harvey's evidence, that the destruction of the traditional forms of New England township government should have led to a powerful sense of disenchantment which the revolutionary movement could have effectively channelled? Furthermore, it must once again be stressed that because of the absence of suitable means of communication, the Halifax government found it extremely difficult to force its will upon the various isolated settlements. Nevertheless, in spite of the questions that can be raised regarding Harvey's interpretation, he successfully introduced a new perspective for viewing Nova Scotia's response to the Revolution.

6 J. B. BREBNER (1937)
THE BREBNER SYNTHESIS

No historian has written as perceptively and authoritatively about Seventeenth and Eighteenth Century Nova Scotia as J. B. Brebner. His Neutral Yankees of Nova Scotia, *published in 1937, took full advantage of the various studies on Nova Scotia and the Revolution published earlier in the decade. Brebner's conclusions were not necessarily original but his general synthesis of secondary and primary material was brilliantly executed.*

The statement, which has frequently been made, that Nova Scotia was saved for the British Crown by the recall of Francis Legge, has little more to recommend it than the surviving assertions of the small group in Halifax who successfully fought him to preserve their fortunes. The response of so peculiar an entity (or nonentity) as Nova Scotia to revolution in North America should not be explained away simply in terms of Legge's two-and-a-half-year campaign of reform. He was unquestionably stupid and apt in making enemies. Yet, had he continued as resident Governor, his enemies could not have gone much further than the hints and warnings of revolution which they had used in bringing him down, because in their assault they had committed themselves and their followers almost irrevocably to a loyalism more fervent than his. Moreover, Halifax with its palace revolutions was not Nova Scotia. About 90 percent of the people were obsessed with their local problems elsewhere. Clearly the explanations for Nova

Scotian behavior, active and passive, must be sought in the persistent peculiarities of the Province itself, of its peoples, and of the positions in which both were placed by the actions of Great Britain and of some of her American Colonies.

It would be a tedious and largely unprofitable task to set Nova Scotian behavior in detail over against the many elements of behavior which historians have arranged in various hypotheses to explain rebellion in other Colonies. Yet a few of these comparisons are valuable. Take, for instance, the thesis that the Colonial merchants, engaged after the Seven Years' War in keen competition with the British mercantile system, roused an American radicalism which grew too strong for them to restrain later when they wanted to restrain it. At once the flat difference emerges that by and large Nova Scotian merchants were in no position to fight British mercantilism. Nova Scotia was by nature nearly the perfect colony according to the mercantilist theory. It produced raw and semimanufactured materials and consumed British manufactured goods. Unlike New England and the Middle Colonies, it had little liquid capital, almost no industry or carrying trade, and nothing approaching the profitable triangular commercial exchange which other Colonies carried on with Europe, Africa and the West Indies. Nova Scotian products entered this trade abundantly, but they were carried almost exclusively by British and New England enterprisers, for Nova Scotia was a 'colony' to both. It might almost be fair to say that Nova Scotia's one important industry, Mauger's rum monopoly, was the chief obstacle to the development of a direct trade with the fishermen and the West Indies because of the protective tariff on rum, although serious Nova Scotian deficiencies as a supply base for grain and flour also entered the picture. There were competitive mercantile profits to be made by serving as an entrepôt in the great smuggling trade with the foreign West Indies, Europe itself, and St. Pierre and Miquelon, by which the other Colonies remedied a little the outward drain of specie to Great Britain. Nova Scotia played this game sufficiently to alarm both the London authorities and Governors Campbell and Legge, but insufficiently to set up its economy on that base. Moreover, smuggling was such a labyrinthine affair, involving Nova Scotian officials and, in the matter of molasses, even Nova Scotian distillers, that it would be absurd to expect public Nova Scotian policy to emerge from it. . . .

Nevertheless, the very elements seemed to combine against any heartening sense of solidarity in overt, rebellious action. Everyone felt that something more than the mere difficulties of frontier life prevented Nova Scotia from being prosperous. It might be the tricky salary takers and law makers at Halifax, but perhaps the men of other Colonies were right in blaming their more powerful prototypes in London. But how could Nova Scotians learn about these matters and discuss them together? An occasional newspaper could help, and the crews of visiting fishing and trading schooners were fairly bursting to impart the pros and cons of the arguments which were the main business of life elsewhere. Yet the sea and the forest lay between Nova Scotia and the core of activity; she was more remote than Nantucket and about as remote as Bermuda. It was impossible to feel and remain convinced of being bound up in the same fateful train of events.

There was not even a sense of solidarity in Nova Scotia. Settlements were scattered at intervals along the edges of a long, narrow peninsula whose rough surface defied the road makers. The unpredictable sea was the road between settlements. There were long stretches of uninhabited forest along the shores all the way from Canso to Annapolis Basin. Annapolis and Granville were separated from Wilmot and Cornwallis by an unprofitable barren. The south shore of Minas basin was fairly solidly occupied, but empty speculative grants lay between Newport and Truro, and one traveled by ferry from Windsor to Partridge island on the way to Fort Cumberland and the isthmus townships. Mere paths reached through the Cobequid mountains from Truro to Tatamagouche and Pictou. There simply could not be an integral Nova Scotia.

Perhaps, then, the principal clue to Nova Scotian behavior in this, as in many other problematical situations, lies in her insulation from the rest of North America. The northeastward trend of the coast, the Appalachian uplands of Maine and New Brunswick, the deep invasion of the Bay of Fundy, push her outward toward Newfoundland and Europe from the main body of North America. Nova Scotia has always had to contemplate the possibility that she may be in North America but not of it, and this mold of circumstances has pressed with varying weight on some generations of Nova Scotians to modify their traditional loyalties and inclinations. France and England, New France and New England, tried to exploit her during the seventeenth century without accepting the responsibility for continuous reinforcement and aid to the inhabitants. In 1710 New England and Old found it imperative to conquer her, but again their support was an intermittent and barely adequate counter to the efforts of France and New France. Her people of that day, the Acadians, had made the land support and increase them, but they were mere pawns in international politics. Small wonder, then, that their one persistent aim from 1710 to 1755, when it sealed their fates, was to be, and to be generally accepted as, neutrals—'the neutral French.' Small wonder, too, that after a brief flurry of conflicting aims in 1775, Nova Scotians a bare fifteen years out of New England naturally and almost inevitably, when confronted by the Revolution, made the same plea.

All in all, both external and domestic circumstances operated to dilute very considerably in Nova Scotia the clash of opinion which prevailed elsewhere. It is now generally believed that in most of the thirteen rebellious American Colonies the majority of the population was passive, but that the radicals formed the larger of the two active minorities and thereby involved their communities. As events proved, the majority in Nova Scotia was also passive, and neither minority was able to rouse its members beyond individual acts or minor joint enterprises for or against Government. . . .

With the probable exception of Halifax, the available evidence demonstrates the quite natural refusal of most Nova Scotians to risk becoming involved in fratricidal strife with the rebellious Colonies. Inevitably this attitude was interpreted by the official loyalists as being synonymous with treason to Great Britain and with the desire actively to assist the rebels. The resident officials of a colony who had vigorously represented it to be ultra-loyal were loath to allow this embarrassing belief to reach London, but such persons as Legge, Gibbons, and various naval or military officers felt no such compunctions. Yet it is permissible to doubt the many assertions that Nova Scotians' sympathy with the revolutionaries was so great that only their own weaknesses prevented them from joining the America Revolution. In all parts of the Province, outside of Halifax, there were a few men who did participate in the Revolution by emigrating or by conspiring at home to aid the rebels and overthrow British authority. They appear to have been distinctly more numerous and more active than the similarly scattered minority who had the courage actively to assist Great Britain. But both groups were negligible as compared with the mass of Nova Scotians, whose former affiliations and present environment put them in the paradoxical position of being positive only in a negative action. They refused to fight their blood brothers, even, as we shall see, to the point of failing in their professed willingness to defend their homes against them. They felt incapable, even when they were willing, to take overt action to destroy British control. They were desperately concerned by the interruption in their economic intercourse with New England. The Nova Scotian settlers were weak and exposed, and knowing this, like the Acadians whom they had supplanted, asked that the belligerents treat them as neutrals. . . .

Clearly no summary phrase can be adequate to explain the behavior of so unintegrated a province. Pensioned Halifax might be another New York for loyalism, but, like New York, she was separated from the rest of her Province by more than geographical factors. Her habitual subservience to London, given explicit outward form by commitments made in the campaign against Legge, had been crystallized by war prosperity, by the presence of the navy and the army, and by the stories of the Loyalist refugees. Opposition at the capital was driven underground. Against this stand the sympathizers with rebellion among the outlying population could make no headway because their friends in the rebellious Colonies had no navy and because they themselves could not assemble from the scattered settlements an effective force for unassisted revolt. Neither the 'Boston Massacre' of March, 1770, nor the blood shed at Lexington five years later, could arouse the general body of New Englanders in Nova Scotia to solidarity or to emulation of the efforts of those who were somewhat similarly placed in New Hampshire and Georgia. This apathy can be attributed to poverty about as much as to the topographical barriers between the settlements. Economically Nova Scotia could neither stand alone nor maintain an effective alliance with New England. She could not even afford to be properly represented in her own Assembly. In her dependence, she completed her gradual progress out of New England's orbit into Great Britain's. The general North American tide of migration had turned west. New England, having received what she thought she wanted most at the peace settlement in the St. Croix boundary and in access to the North Atlantic fisheries, released her already weakened grip. To use a generalization so broad as to be almost meaningless without corroborative detail, Nova Scotia had insulated and neutralized the New England migrants so thoroughly that as Nova Scotians they had henceforth to look eastward to London for direction and help rather than southwestward to Boston as they had done in the past.*

7 M. W. ARMSTRONG (1946)
NEUTRALITY AND RELIGION

In his analysis of Nova Scotia during the Revolution, J. B. Brebner, like his predecessors, failed to discuss the impact of the "Great Awakening" upon the colony. Aware of the significance of the religious revival, Professor M. W. Armstrong felt compelled to ask the question, "Was there any direct relationship between the revival and neutrality?" His answer, though not entirely convincing, nevertheless must be seriously considered as a possible major reason for Nova Scotia's neutrality during the early years of the Revolution.

Hitherto, little attention has been paid to the fact that in Nova Scotia the years of the Revolution coincided exactly with a revival of religion which swept through every New England settlement in the province with the most far-reaching and profound social and spiritual results. Such a widespread and vital movement was bound to exert an influence upon Nova Scotians' attitude towards the Revolution. The extent of that influence and the interaction of neutrality and religion have yet to be estimated, but there can be little doubt that the two were at least mutually dependent, and that the 'Great Awakening' in Nova Scotia was an expression of democratic ideals and spiritual independence which shows that these sons of New England were neither so mercenary nor so lethargic as they may at first appear. . . .

Cut off from New England (in 1775 and 1776) with little chance of refilling their pulpits or recuperating their losses in membership and wealth, the outlook of Nova Scotian Congregationalism must have seemed particularly dark. . . .

---

* Brebner, *The Neutral Yankees of Nova Scotia*, pp. 291-293, 298-300, 313-314, 352-353.

It was to people in this discouraging situation, faced with the loss of their religion in addition to being 'divided betwixt natural Affection to our nearest Relations, and good Faith and Friendship to our King and Country' that the revival of religion offered at once an escape and a vindication. . . .

Such emphasis on 'spiritual' interests and such wide spread preoccupation with other worldly affairs was bound to have an influence upon Nova Scotians' attitude towards the Revolution. The colonial question necessarily appeared less important as men's minds placed more and more value upon 'heavenly' things. After all, in the light of eternity what comparison was there between the claims of King George and the claims of King Jesus? In 1775 Henry Alline himself refused the offer of a commission in the militia, preferring as he said, 'a Commission from Heaven to go forth and enlist my fellow mortals to fight under the banner of King Jesus.' One searches his *Journal* in vain for any evidence of interest in political affairs. Even on the two occasions when he was captured by American privateers, his only response was to warn 'them that wish well to their souls' to 'flee from privateers as they would from the jaws of hell, for methinks a privateer may be called a floating hell.' Similarly, when addressing a company of soldiers at Liverpool in November 1782, he limited himself to warning them against the evils of profanity.

To assume, therefore, that while their brothers in the Thirteen Colonies were engaged in a life and death struggle for the high ideals of 'Life, Liberty and the pursuit of Happiness,' Nova Scotians were unmoved by any higher considerations than safety and profits is unfair. Indeed, the Great Awakening itself may be considered to have been a retreat from the grim realities of the world to the safety and pleasantly exciting warmth of the revival meeting, and to profits and rewards of another character. Although this psychological law of compensation undoubtedly played a part in the eagerness with which Alline's doctrines were accepted by his countrymen, it is not the whole explanation of their conduct. Besides the possibilities for release offered by the revival to emotionally starved and mentally perplexed people, there was also a large element of self-assertion and revolt in the movement. The Reverend Jonathan Scott of Chebogue, the doughty champion of 'Old Light' Congregationalism against the inroads of the revivalists, complained bitterly that in his congregation the awakening had meant insubordination to the authority of the church. Members of his parish, 'rejected all his Reasonings with Indignation and Contempt.' They talked loudly of their 'Christian Liberty,' and complained bitterly of any 'restraining and infringing' upon it. Such 'liberty' was the very essence of Henry Alline's preaching; indeed, it gave rise to the accusation of antinomianism which was hurled at him during his lifetime and which continued to be applied to his followers long after his death. . . .

The emotional extravangances of the enthusiasts and the lengths to which they carried their peculiar beliefs in 'Christian Liberty' were the subject of constant criticism by their opponents, yet even these may be interpreted as the exaggerated assertions of personal independence. Such excesses as crawling about like wild beasts, disturbing and disrupting services of worship, and speaking with new tongues, were psychologically primitive traits, but they were also the marks of men and women who refused to conform to contemporary standards and wished to demonstrate their own alliance with a power which was superior to all human conventions. The same individualism which found expressions in other molds in the Thirteen Colonies, activated the religious extraverts to the northern outpost.

Negatively, an escape from fear and divided loyalties; positively, an assertion of democratic ideals and a determination to maintain them, the Great Awakening in Nova Scotia gave self-respect and satisfaction to people whose economic and political position was both humiliating and distressing. . . .

In comparison with the physical and economic factors which held the province within the British Empire, 'the Great Reformation under Mr. Henry Alline,' may seem insignificant and remote, yet psychologically it played a part. Not only Mr. Alline, but lesser exhorters in every township pointed out the blessings of peace and turned men's minds away from the political issues of the day. In a state of divided loyalties and impotence the Neutral Yankees found an indirect method of asserting their independence. Political neutrality was superseded by religious enthusiasm.*

---

* M. W. Armstrong, "Neutrality and Religion in Revolutionary Nova Scotia," *The New England Quarterly* (March 1946), 51, 53, 54, 57-58, 60-61, 62.

8 S. D. CLARK (1959)
THE FRONTIER THESIS

Frederick Jackson Turner's frontier thesis has exerted a considerable impact upon North American historiography. But it was not until 1959, that the Turner thesis was applied in a sophisticated manner to Nova Scotia during the early years of the Revolution. However, it was a sociologist, S. D. Clark, rather than a historian who undertook the study. He viewed Nova Scotia's reactions as one of many genuine "Movements of Political Protest in Canada." He argued that

In terms of the kinds of movements which grew up, there was no essential difference between Canada and the United States. Developing as the frontier of the United States did through the spread of settlement into the interior of the continent, the Canadian frontier offered as fertile a field for the growth of movements of a radical or revolutionary character. As across the border, these movements were essentially separatist, anti-authoritarian in character. They grew out of the feelings of isolated people that their problems were peculiar to themselves and could only be solved through their own efforts. . . .*

In his analysis of developments in Nova Scotia in 1775 and 1776, Clark maintained that there was a strong revolutionary movement in the colony. However, this movement, largely due to the isolated nature of the Nova Scotian settlements and the existing military realities, was channelled into the religious revival. Clark thus used the well-worn historical tool, the Turner frontier thesis, to strengthen the conclusion reached earlier by Armstrong.

When war came it could scarcely by expected that the people of Nova Scotia would remain aloof. Geographically, economically, culturally, the community of Nova Scotia was a part of the larger New England community. Certainly, in the St. John Valley and east to the Isthmus of Chignecto the forces favouring enlistment on the revolutionary side were little less strong than they were in Machias or further west. The people were almost all New Englanders, and no geographical barrier cut them off from their fellow-countrymen. The land frontier of Massachusetts extended un-

---

* S. D. Clark, *Movements of Political Protest in Canada 1640-1840* (Toronto: University of Toronto Press, 1959), p. 6.

broken along the coast and about the north shore of the Bay of Fundy. South, from the Isthmus of Chignecto to the head of Cobequid Bay, geography linked the population almost as closely to the mainland settlements stretching back to Machias and Penobscot. Recruits for Eddy's rebel army were secured as far down as Londonderry, Onslow, and Pictou.

Though the geographical ties were not quite as close, the settlements along the South Shore and up the Annapolis Valley were just as much a part of New England's frontier as were those on the mainland. Stretching north and east along the coast of Nova Scotia, such fishing villages as Yarmouth, Barrington, and Liverpool were only separated by an easy stretch of water from such fishing villages as Salem, Gloucester, and Newburyport, extending north and east along the Massachusetts coast. Isolated from one another and from Halifax by land, these communities and those up the Annapolis Valley were closely linked to the New England mainland by trade and by the constant movement of people back and forth attending to matters of business or family affairs. The extent of the network of business and personal relationships was evident in Perkins' day-to-day conduct of his affairs as recorded in his diary.

To the people of Nova Scotia the question at issue in the revolution was largely that of their relationship with New England. The plea of the inhabitants of Yarmouth that they be allowed to remain neutral in the war represented truly their position. They had no positive desire to break free from Britain. What they were concerned about was that they should not be cut off from New England. The forces at work in 1776 were essentially the same forces which earlier had led the Acadians to seek a position of neutrality. Dependence upon the New England tie compelled the population of Nova Scotia to seek to stay outside any imperial system which threatened its severance. With the outbreak of war in 1775 between Britain and the English colonies, opposition to the Militia Act, smuggling and, on the mainland, open rebellion offered themselves as the only way by which the people of Nova Scotia could maintain the vital link with New England.

Closely related to the connection with New England as a force determining the position of Nova Scotia in the revolution was the intense localism of the village communities. British authority, as represented by the government in Halifax, constituted a direct threat to the right of these communities to govern their own affairs.

To them, as a result, independence in 1775 meant not so much the freedom of the colonies from interference by the motherland as freedom of the local community from interference by colonial governments. Like all frontier people, the Nova Scotians were separatists. Compelled to act on their own, and dependent largely on their own resources, they had no strong interest in the affairs of the state. In this attitude of mind, the American revolutionary movement of independence had strong roots in Nova Scotia.

To the extent that a military effort was made to free Nova Scotia from British rule it secured its support very largely from this spirit of local independence. The driving force behind the attempted invasion of the province came from the settlements in that no man's land between Nova Scotia and Massachusetts where the population felt no strong attachment to any political authority. The people of Machias acted almost as much against the authority of the Continental Congress as against that of the British Parliament. Indeed, on the whole periphery of the American community, the revolution assumed much of this character of local uprisings of the population directed against all outside authority. So long, however, as the war was a struggle to free the population of America from British rule (rather than a struggle to strengthen the political authority of the United Colonies), it received important support from local uprisings. It was because of this close relationship between local movements of independence and the larger movement of colonial independence that such developments as the increase of smuggling, the holding of town meetings, and the Newlight religious revival assumed such importance in Nova Scotia.

In the end, political authority in Nova Scotia received its strongest challenge not from the military efforts of the rebels but from the much more widespread religious uprising of the populace. From the commencement of the revolution the leaders of the Congregational churches in Nova Scotia had shown a strong sympathy for the cause of the rebels. At least three of the Congregational ministers in the province returned to New England after the outbreak of hostilities, one to serve as a chaplain in the revolutionary army; and one other found himself in trouble with the authorities in Halifax for seditious preaching. The strong separatist spirit of Congregationalism offered support to the movement of local independence within the Nova Scotia village settlements while its strong New England roots favoured its close identification with the interests of the rebelling colonies. Nonconformity bred an attitude of political dissent. 'I am sorry to tell your Lordship,' Massey wrote the Secretary of State, November 22, 1772, of the inhabitants of Nova Scotia, 'they are as well inclined to be Rebellious, as any part of the Continent, and . . . until Presbytery is drove out of his Majesty's Dominions, Rebellion will ever continue, nor will that set ever submit to the Laws of old England.' On December 31, Massey wrote again, 'If some test to keep the desenting Clergy in order be not devised; you may depend upon it; his Majesty will hardly ever experience a faithful Subject in the whole Massachusettes, nor in this province of that persuasion.'

What intellectual leadership there was in Nova Scotia before 1776 was largely provided by the nine or so Congregational ministers in the colony. Already, however, before the outbreak of revolution, such leadership had been seriously weakened by the emergence of a powerful evangelistic movement within the Congregational churches, and with the disturbances of revolution the formal organization of Congregationalism rapidly disintegrated. The rise of the Newlight movement in 1776 was a reflection of the collapse of the traditional leadership of the Nova Scotia village communities and the development of a great mass movement of social protest.

Maintenance of close proprietory control over the early settlement of New Englanders in Nova Scotia had emphasized the character of the village structure as a 'closed social system,' but unrest in New England, evident in the Great Awakening in religion and in local movements of political protest, made its effects felt in the new frontier communities of Nova Scotia. The people who moved to the frontier were the people least socially accommodated within their home communities, and efforts to impose upon them the kind of controls from which they were seeking an escape met with vigorous resistance. Squatter settlement constituted more of a challenge to local proprietory control than to the control of the governing authorities in Halifax; indeed, early protests against interferences from Halifax with the government of the local villages reflected as much a concern on the part of local proprietory interests to check the growth of a free land philosophy developing out of the conditions of frontier settlement as a concern on the part of the people at large to preserve their democratic rights.

Impoverished and without leadership of its own, the great

mass of the population could offer no effective resistance to the system of control being imposed upon it. Random individual protests against authority, evident in occasional refusals to conform to the rigid Puritan code of morals, the development of an attitude of shiftlessness and general irresponsibility, and, in the more isolated areas, the growth of a spirit of lawlessness, reflected an underlying social philosophy of nonconformity which weakened the sense of solidarity of the village community but provided no positive force of social reorganization. Development of such a force of social reorganization came with the rise of the Newlight movement of religious revival.

The outbreak of war between Britain and the English colonies had revealed the weaknesses of the local village social structure dependent upon leadership provided by New England. Unable to join up local movements of independence with the larger movement of colonial independence, many of those individuals within the Nova Scotian villages, Congregational ministers and others, in the best position to provide leadership, returned to New England, while many others like Perkins in Liverpool, anxious to protect important business investments or claims to political office, could offer only half-hearted support to the revolutionary cause. The Newlight religious revival shifted the movement of social protest to the level of the masses. By developing a purely local leadership, it freed the Nova Scotian village settlements from the close dependence upon the New England tie, while, at the same time, it strengthened enormously the spirit of local autonomy and resistance to Halifax rule. The strong other-worldly attitude of mind which it cultivated reflected faithfully the frontiersman's dislike of political authority and lack of interest in political affairs, while the Newlight belief that only people who had secured faith would be saved justified the frontiersman's natural disregard of social distinctions based upon wealth or class. To the extent that it won the support of the population, what the Newlight movement secured was the social reorganization of the Nova Scotia village communities, weakened by the disturbances resulting from settlement in a new country, the pressures of conflicting economic and political interests, and the rigidities of a social-religious structure which had hardened over its years of development in New England.

The weakening support of the established Church of England

and the strengthening of democratic, equalitarian principles of social organization were a direct consequence of the Newlight revival in religion. Newlightism represented a protest against traditionalism, against authority as it was established in the state and the church. It was thus an expression of the levelling forces of the frontier. 'The fanaticism of this country,' Rev. W. Ellis wrote from Windsor, September 14, 1776, of the Newlights about him, 'will never produce Heroes, like Barebones and his fellows, it is sly and selfish, and a piece of that levelling principle which pervades this whole Continent, as they are impatient of superiority in rank and condition, so they are offended that men should be sent on purpose to instruct them, who are all wise and learned in their own opinion.'

Yet there developed out of Newlight religious teaching no clearly formulated social or political philosophy. Rather, an ignorance of social or political questions tended to be characteristic of the Newlight religious following. It was, however, in this very cultivation of an attitude of ignorance or indifference to social and political questions that the influence of Newlightism gained much of its political significance. Ignorance of political issues constituted one of the strongest defences of the Nova Scotian out-settlements against political exploitation. In a community such as Nova Scotia in 1775 political organization (and social organization in general) clearly favoured those persons and groups located closest to the seats of power. The people in the out-settlements, by the very force of circumstances, could have little voice in government. At best, therefore, the most they could do was 'co-operate' with the government, and for such co-operation an understanding of political issues, of what the government was trying to do, was essential. Conversely, one highly effective means these people had of resisting government was that of simply failing to understand what government was trying to do. An ignorant population, from one point of view, may be an easy population to govern, but from another point of view, it can be an exceedingly difficult one. Ignorance of political affairs, of course, was not a consequence of Newlight religious teaching. Rather, it was an almost inevitable consequence of conditions of frontier life as they were to be found in Nova Scotia at that time. The significance of the Newlight religious revival as a revolutionary force in the community lay, however, in its effect in intensifying and strengthening such ignorance.

The Newlight religious community, in a sense, seceded from the larger political community and developed complete within itself a social world of its own. Here within the religious revival was to be found the fullest expression of that spirit of local independence which permeated the whole American revolutionary movement. In its intense separatism, Newlightism constituted a more serious challenge to established political authority than did any of the more purely political manifestations of social protest. Only smuggling, perhaps, in the Nova Scotia out-settlements gained as great importance as a force of resistance to the state. Like religious revivalism, smuggling found support in and in turn strengthened the population's lack of regard for its obligations to the political community. It was an equally clear manifestation of an attitude of 'bad' citizenship.

The widespread growth of political sympathy for the American revolutionary cause, together with the rise of the Newlight religious revival, offered an indication of the extent of the social unrest of the outlying population in Nova Scotia in the years immediately preceding the outbreak of the war between Britain and the English colonies. Growing resentment against the rule of the narrow governing party in Halifax strengthened the sense of solidarity of the village communities and gave to the town meeting a new importance as a vehicle for the expression of local discontent. On the other hand, the weakening social position of local village and church leaders reflected the strength of democratic influences growing out of the conditions of frontier settlement and emphasized the importance of the Newlight religious revival as a force of social reorganization. Though the Cumberland rebels were defeated by the forces of the Crown, and Allan and Eddy were driven from the province, the spirit of revolt which found expression in religious revival could not so easily be crushed. The revolutionary movement in Nova Scotia was rooted in the strong separatist attitude of mind of the outlying fishing and farming population and that attitude of mind survived the military and political developments of the revolution though the province remained, by the fortunes of war, a part of the British Empire.*

---

* *Ibid.*, pp. 69-74

C. CRITICAL SUMMARY

Without question, the isolation of the settlements of Nova Scotia, the British Navy and the "Great Awakening" all help to explain why Nova Scotia did not join the Revolution. M. W. Armstrong and J. B. Brebner provide the most convincing answers available to this often perplexing question. Nothing of consequence has been written in the past twenty years to challenge their respective points of view.

It should, however, be stressed that there is much serious historical work still to be done in order to understand Nova Scotia's early response to the Revolution. For example, Armstrong's thesis must be carefully examined in order to see whether the "Great Awakening" really had any impact on Nova Scotia in 1775 and 1776. The religious revival certainly was of consequence after *1776. Armstrong, however, has not presented a convincing case for the crucial year 1775 and 1776.*

Moreover, there are a few rather important gaps in Brebner's general thesis. He has not fully explained either the weakness of the New England thrust into Nova Scotia in 1775 and 1776 or the disastrous effects of New England privateering upon the revolutionary movement in the colony. By 1775 it is clear that most "Yankees" no longer considered Nova Scotia to be "New England's Outpost." This significant change in attitude had taken place after the Louisbourg Expedition of 1745. During the Seven Years' War period and afterwards, New England leaders turned towards the interior of North America for strategic economic and imperialistic reasons. A sophisticated analysis and explanation of this shift of interest is absolutely vital in order to understand New England's attitude towards Nova Scotia in 1775 and 1776.*

Brebner also failed to emphasize adequately the key role played by New England privateers in keeping the potentially rebellious Nova Scotian communities isolated from one another during the crucial months of 1775 and 1776. Had these communities been in close touch with events in Massachusetts and had they

---

* The most recent study does not adequately deal with these two important issues. See J. H. Ahlin, *Maine Rubicon: Downeast Settlers during the American Revolution* (Calais: Calais Advertiser Press, 1966).

been aware of the existence of revolutionary sentiment elsewhere in Nova Scotia, things might have been different in the colony. But the aggressive Yankee privateers only strengthened the prevailing sense of isolation and destroyed any possible effective collective movement. In addition, the privateers, by their depredations, further weakened the revolutionary movement in Nova Scotia.

Many hitherto unanswered questions concerning Nova Scotia and the Revolution will be answered when perceptive regional studies are written. These studies will have to take into consideration recent American scholarship and place the Nova Scotian region, whether Halifax or Cumberland or the Annapolis Valley, not only in its proper Nova Scotian context but also in its proper North American context. More must be known about those men in Nova Scotia who supported the revolutionary cause and about those who were vociferously opposed to it. The general significance of the emigration of New England leaders from Nova Scotia before 1776 should also be seriously studied. It is to be hoped that, in the not too distant future, regional and biographical studies will clarify Nova Scotia's response to the American Revolution in 1775 and 1776.

PART TWO

Why did Quebec refuse to join the American Revolution in 1775-76?

INTRODUCTION

*By early autumn of 1775 General George Washington had decided that it was essential to strike quickly and boldly at the colony of Quebec. There were at least three major reasons for such a decision. Firstly, Washington and the Continental Congress had been persuaded that a surprising number of French Canadians were sympathetic to the aims of Congress. Secondly, it was felt that Quebec had to be captured in order to prevent a powerful British expedition against the Americans in the spring of 1776, and also to discourage possible Indian raids. Thirdly, there was a strong "imperialistic" drive—a desire to absorb the considerable economic potential of the St. Lawrence-Great Lakes System.**

Despite the fact that the American army was still poorly organized by September 1775, a two-pronged offensive was directed against Quebec. One American column, under the command of Richard Montgomery, moved up the Hudson-Lake Champlain-Richelieu corridor, while the other, under Benedict Arnold, travelled by way of the Kennebec River wilderness route. The French-Canadian inhabitants, together with the growing English-speaking population had been made ready for the invasion by propaganda prepared by Washington and other military leaders.

1 GENERAL PHILIP SCHUYLER (1775) LETTER TO THE INHABITANTS OF CANADA

Friends And Countrymen: The Various causes that have drove the ancient *British* Colonies in *America* to arms have been so fully set

---

* R. W. Van Alstyne, *The Rising American Empire* (Oxford: Basil Blackwell, 1960), pp. 37-40.

forth in the several petitions, papers, letters, and declarations, published by the Grand Congress, that our *Canadian* brethren (at the extirpation of whose liberty as well as ours the nefarious schemes of a cruel Ministry directly tend) cannot fail of being informed thereof, and pleased that the Grand Congress have ordered an Army into *Canada*, to expel from thence, if possible, those *British* Troops, which, now acting under the orders of a despotic Ministry, would wish to enslave their countrymen. This measure, necessary as it is, the Congress would not have entered on, but in the fullest confidence that it would be perfectly agreeable to you; for, judging of your feelings by their own, they could not conceive that any thing but the force of necessity could induce you tamely to bear the insult and ignominy that is daily imposed on you, or that you could calmly sit by, and see those chains forging which are intended to bind you, your posterity, and ours, in one common and eternal slavery; to secure you and ourselves from such a dreadful bondage, to prevent the effects that might follow from Ministerial Troops remaining in *Canada*, to restore to you those rights which every subject of the *British* Empire, from the highest to the very lowest order, or whatever his religious sentiments may be, is entitled to, are the only views of the Congress.*

2 GEORGE WASHINGTON (1775)
PROCLAMATION TO THE INHABITANTS OF CANADA

Friends and Brethren: The unnatural contest between the *English* Colonies and *Great Britain* has now risen to such a height that arms alone must decide it. The Colonies, confiding in the justice of their cause and the purity of their intentions, have reluctantly appealed to that Being in whose hands are all human events. He has hitherto smiled upon their virtuous efforts. The hand of tyranny has been arrested in its ravages, and the *British* arms, which have shone with so much splendour in every part of the globe, are now tarnished with disgrace and disappointment. Generals of approved experience, who boasted of subduing this great Continent, find themselves circumscribed within the limits of a single City and its suburbs, suffering all the shame and distress of a siege, while the freeborn sons of *America*, animated by the genuine principles of

---

* P. Force, Philip Schuyler to the Inhabitants of Canada, September 5, 1775, *American Archives,* Fourth Series (Washington, 1840), III, pp. 671-672.

liberty and love of their Country, with increasing union, firmness, and discipline, repel every attack, and despise every danger. Above all, we rejoice that our enemies have been deceived with regard to you; they have persuaded themselves, they have even dared to say, that the *Canadians* were not capable of distinguishing between the blessings of liberty and the wretchedness of slavery; that gratifying the vanity of a little circle of nobility would blind the eyes of the people of *Canada*; by such artifices they hoped to bend you to their views, but they have been deceived; instead of finding in you that poverty of soul and baseness of spirit, they see, with a chagrin equal to our joy, that you are enlightened, generous, and virtuous; that you will not renounce your own rights, or serve as instruments to deprive your fellow-subjects of theirs.

Come, then, my brethren, unite with us in an indissoluable union; let us run together to the same goal. We have taken up arms in defence of our liberty, our property, our wives, and our children; we are determined to preserve them or die. We look forward with pleasure to that day, not far remote, we hope, when the inhabitants of *America* shall have one sentiment, and the full enjoyment of the blessings of a free Government. Incited by these motives, and encouraged by the advice of many friends of liberty among you, the grand *American* Congress have sent an Army into your Province, under the command of General *Schuyler*, not to plunder, but to protect you; to animate and bring forth into action those sentiments of freedom you have disclosed, and which the tools of despotism would extinguish through the whole creation. To cooperate with this design, and to frustrate those cruel and perfidious schemes which would deluge our frontiers with the blood of women and children, I have detached Colonel *Arnold* into your Country, with a part of the Army under my command. I have enjoined upon him, and I am certain that he will consider himself, and act as in the Country of his patrons and best friends. Necessaries and accommodations of every kind which you may furnish he will thankfully receive, and render the full value. I invite you, therefore, as friends and brethren, to provide him with such supplies as your Country affords; and I pledge myself not only for your safety and security, but for ample compensation. Let no man desert his habitation. Let no one flee as before an enemy. The cause of *America* and of liberty is the cause of every virtuous *American* citizen, whatever may be his religion or his descent. The

United Colonies know no distinction but such as slavery, corruption, and arbitrary domination, may create. Come, then, ye generous citizens, range yourselves under the standard of general liberty, against which all the force and artifice of tyranny will never be able to prevail.*

American propaganda did not succeed in winning a large number of English- or French-speaking inhabitants to the revolutionary cause. Of course, the clergy and seigneurs, impressed by the terms of the Quebec Act, vociferously opposed the invaders from the beginning. The English-speaking merchants, on the other hand, were at first confused and most of them did not support the British until they realized how completely dependent they were on London for their economic survival. However, most of the habitants, *indeed the majority of the population, though they were unable to grasp the principles underlying the revolutionary movement and in spite of their deep suspicion of American motives, gave the invaders a favourable reception. There was little dancing in the streets, of course, but there was nevertheless a widespread sympathy for the Americans, especially when the* habitants *received high prices in specie for their agricultural produce and other services. One American volunteer observed on November 3, 1775:*

The *Canadians*, in general, on this side of the St. Lawrence, are very friendly to us, almost unanimously so along the River Sorel. . . . More hospitable people I never saw; you cannot enter into a peasant's house, at any time of day, but they immediately set a loaf of bread and a pan of milk before you.†

Another American noted later in November:

The Canadians are, in general, favourable to the Americans. . . . They received them [*the invaders*] into their houses, bring them provisions, and seem well pleased with their guests.††

Too many Americans, in 1775, were eager to equate French-Canadian hospitality and seeming sympathy with enthusiastic and unqualified support for the American cause. As in Nova Scotia, the evidence suggests that most French Canadians—although sym-

---

* *Ibid.*, Washington to the Inhabitants of Canada, 1775, p. 764.
† *Ibid.*, ? to ?, November 3, 1775, p. 1342.
††*Ibid.*, "An Account of the State of Quebec etc." [At the en dof November, 1775], p. 1724.

pathetic to the invaders at the beginning largely for economic and strategic reasons—were nevertheless content to adopt a policy of neutrality until it was clear which side would win. But their neutral posture was such only in the military sense. If they had refused to supply food to the Americans, the invaders would never have reached the St. Lawrence. There was, however, a small minority of habitants *led by priests and a few seigneurs who violently opposed the Americans. The small number that was willing to join the invaders in their military adventures never amounted to more than a few hundred. There were three similar groups in the English-speaking population but it should be emphasized that, in all probability, most of the merchants, after much soul-searching, supported the British since they did not wish to see the Americans gain control of the "Commercial Empire of the St. Lawrence."*

It seems clear that in 1775 the vast majority of the inhabitants of Quebec, were content to walk the knife-edge of neutrality. When, in the following year, the Americans showed themselves incapable of retaining control of most of the colony and began to mistreat the inhabitants, the invaders lost whatever sympathy they had once possessed. With the arrival of British reinforcements in the spring of 1776, the American cause in Canada was lost.

A. CONTEMPORARY OPINION

1 GOVERNOR FREDERICK HALDIMAND (1780)
THE QUEBEC ACT

Haldimand, who in 1778 succeeded Guy Carleton as Governor of Quebec, agreed with his predecessor that the Quebec Act had saved Quebec.

As it is my Duty, it has been my Business to inform myself of the State of the Country & I coincide with the Majority of the Legislative Council in Considering the Canadians as the People of the Country, and think that in making Laws and Regulations for the Administration of these Laws, Regard is to be paid to the Sentiments and Manner of thinking of 60,000 rather than of 2,000—three fourths of whom are Traders & Cannot with propriety be Considered as Residents of the Province. In this point of view the Quebec Act, was both just and Politic, tho' unfortunately for the British Empire, it was enacted Ten Years too late—It Requires but Little Penetration to Discover that had the System of Government sollicited by the Old Subjects [*the Americans*] been adopted in Canada, this Colony would in 1775 have become one of the United States of America. Whoever Considers the Number of Old Subjects who in that Year corresponded with and Joined the Rebels . . . must feel this Truth however national or Religious Prejudices will not allow him to declare it.

On the other hand, the Quebec Act alone has prevented or Can in any Degree prevent the Emissaries of France and the Rebellious Colonies from Succeeding in their Efforts to withdraw the Canadian Clergy & Noblesse from their Allegiance to the Crown of Great Britain. . . . This is not the time for Innovations and it Cannot be Sufficiently inculcated on the part of Government that the Quebec Act is a Sacred Charter, granted by the King in Parliament to the Canadians as a Security for their Religion, Laws and Property.*

The Quebec Act certainly helps to explain why the clergy and seigneurs supported the British. But the Act had no profound favourable impact upon the habitants *nor did it win the enthusiastic support of the English-speaking merchants.*

2 JOHN ADAMS AND SAM ADAMS (1776)
THE DECLARATION OF INDEPENDENCE AND QUEBEC

The revolutionary leaders, John and Sam Adams, believed that the decision not to declare independence until July 4, 1776 was largely responsible for Quebec's refusal to join the Revolution. On July 3, 1776, John Adams wrote to his wife:

IF a declaration of independence had been declared seven months ago . . . we would be in possession of Canada. †

Less than two weeks later Sam Adams declared:

If the Declaration had been made nine months earlier Canada would be ours today.††

---

* Haldimand to Germain, October 25, 1786, Public Archives of Canada, B. 54.
† C. F. Adams, ed., Adams to his wife, July 3, 1776, *Familiar Letters of John Adams and his Wife Abigail Smith Adams, during the Revolution* (New York: Hurd and Houghton, 1876), p. 192.
††H. A. Cushing, ed., Samuel Adams to R. H. Leee, July 15, 1776, *The Writings of Samuel Adams* (New York: G. P. Putnam's Sons, 1906), III, p. 297.

Without a Declaration of Independence to guide and inspire them, it was contended that the French Canadians in late 1775 and early 1776 were in no position to understand the true motives of the invaders. Thus the invasion failed to precipitate the kind of widespread popular uprising that both John and Sam Adams were convinced would have resulted if the Declaration of Independence had been made public before the invasion. Both of these men, it appears, were misinformed regarding the mood of Quebec. An earlier Declaration of Independence would not have transformed the widespread neutrality into revolutionary agitation. Most people in Quebec were far more interested in the state of trade or in their crops than in revolutionary ideals!

3 THE CONTINENTAL CONGRESS (1776) MILITARY WEAKNESSES AND BAD LUCK

The Congress took into consideration the report of the committee appointed to enquire into the causes of the miscarriages in Canada, wherein they represent, as their opinion,

'That the short inlistments of the continental troops in Canada, have been one great cause of the miscarriages there, by rendering unstable the number of men engaged in military enterprizes, by making them disorderly and disobedient to their officers, and by precipitating the commanding officers into measures which their prudence might have postponed, could they have relied on a longer continuance of their troops in service:

That the want of hard money has been one other great source of the miscarriages in Canada, rendering the supplies of necessaries difficult and precarious, the establishment of proper magazines absolutely impracticable, and the pay of the troops of little use to them:

That a still greater, and more fatal, source of misfortune has been, the prevalence of the small pox in that army; a great proportion whereof has therby been usually kept unfit for duty.'

With this the Congress concurred.*

---

* C. Ford, ed., *Journals of the Continental Congress 1774-1789* (Washington: U.S. Government Printing Office, 1906), V, pp. 617-618.

4 CHARLES CARROLL (1776)
MILITARY REALITIES AND CANADIAN REACTIONS

In February, 1776, the Continental Congress selected Benjamin Franklin, Samuel Chase and the wealthy Roman Catholic, Charles Carroll, to visit Quebec and to breathe some new life into the American cause. Carroll's observations are extremely penetrating.

It is impossible to give you a just idea of the lowness of the Continental credit here, from want of hard money, and the prejudice it is to our affairs. . . . The general apprehension that we shall be driven out of the Province as soon as the King's troops can arrive, concurs with the frequent breaches of promise the inhabitants have experienced, in determining them to trust our people no further. . . .

Our enemies take the advantage of this distress to make us look contemptible in the eyes of the Canadians, who have been provoked by the violences of our military, in exacting provisions and services from them without pay, a conduct towards a people who suffered us to enter their country as friends, that the most urgent necessity can scarce excuse, since it has contributed much to the changing their good disposition towards us into enmity, and makes them wish our departure.*

5 BISHOP BRIAND (1775)
THE AUTHORITY OF THE CHURCH

For some contemporaries, the most important factor in accounting for Quebec's response to the Revolution was the anti-American policy adopted by Bishop Briand. Without doubt, Briand's influence was of some consequence but it is debatable whether it was the "most important" influencing factor. On May 22, 1775, Briand issued the following mandement:

A troop of subjects in revolt against their lawful Sovereign, who is at the same time ours, have just made an irruption into this province, less in the hope of maintaining themselves here than with a view of dragging you into their revolt or at least preventing you from opposing their pernicious design. The remarkable goodness

---

* K. M. Rowland, *The Life of Charles Carroll of Carrollton 1737-1832* (New York: G. P. Putnam's Sons, 1898), I, pp. 154, 156.

and gentleness with which we have been governed by his very gracious Majesty, King George the Third, since the fortune of war subjected us to his rule; the recent favours with which he has loaded us, in restoring to us the use of our laws and the free exercise of our religion; and in letting us participate in all the privileges and advantages of British subjects, would no doubt be enough to excite your gratitude and zeal in support of the interests of the British Crown. But motives even more urgent must speak to your heart at the present moment. Your oaths, your religion, lay upon you the unavoidable duty of defending your country and your King with all the strength you possess.*

The priests were later instructed to refuse the sacraments to those of their parishioners who overtly supported the Americans.

This "spiritual pressure" probably weakened the revolutionary cause in Quebec but to what extent it is not certain. It must not be forgotten that the habitants *were not puppets in the hands of the priests. The* habitants *were, it is true, closely tied to the Church but long before the Conquest they had developed certain traits of stubborness and independence. These people could and often did think for themselves, sometimes to the consternation of their priests.*

B. NINETEENTH CENTURY VIEWS

1 F. X. GARNEAU (1846)
GRATITUDE FOR ROYAL GRACE

François-Xavier Garneau has been called "French Canada's first scientific historian."† His Histoire du Canada depuis sa découverte jusqu'à nos jours *can still be read with profit. Garneau's early anticlericalism and his deep sympathy for Louis-Joseph Papineau's cause in 1837-38 did not influence in any appreciable manner his analysis of Quebec's response to the American Revolution in 1775 and 1776 .However, Garneau's concern with French-Canadian*

---

* H. Têtu, Mandement of May 22, 1775, *Évêques de Québec* (Quebec: N. S. Hardy, 1889), p. 326. Translation from R. Coupland, *The Quebec Act A Study in Statesmanship* (Oxford: Oxford University Press, 1925), p. 170.

† M. Wade, *The French Canadians 1760-1945* (Toronto: The Macmillan Company of Canada, 1956), p. 287.

ethnic and cultural survival persuaded him that his compatriots would have had far more to lose than to gain by joining the revolutionary cause. It is noteworthy that Garneau contrasted the "apathy" or neutrality of most of the French Canadians with the anti-British sentiment of the English-speaking inhabitants. Garneau distorted somewhat the response of the English-speaking inhabitants to the American invaders in order to emphasize to his Anglophile readers how "loyal" and "British" the habitants *actually were at a crucial time in Quebec's history.*

. . . Meanwhile, scarcely did the governor [*Carleton*] find time to make a survey of the state of the colony, from which he had been absent for several years . . . when his attention was drawn towards the frontiers, and upon the propagandism the Americans were striving to maintain against British sway in Canada, into which copies of the Congress' address had penetrated by several ways simultaneously.

The fine names of 'liberty' and 'national independence' have always a charm for noble minds; a generous spirit is ever moved at their very sound. The polished Parisian, the Swiss herdsman, feel the sacred influence, in common, of proclaimed freedom. The address of the Congress, therefore, despite the recklessness of parts of its strain, caused a great sensation among the Canadian rural populations and the British townsmen. The latter, now no longer hopeful of dominating their fellow colonists of French race, mostly became American partisans. The situation of Carleton was a difficult one at this crisis. Happily for him, the Canadian clergy and seigniors had become firmly bound to British interests through the confirmation of feudal tenures and the recognized right of tithing, two institutions which they could not hope to preserve if a levelling revolution supervened; and with these two orders of men marched the burgess class in the towns, which was as yet, however, neither numerous nor opulent.

Through a fear of jeopardizing their religion and nationality by entering into a confederation both protestant and alien in blood,—an apprehension not groundless, for the men of that confederation had already incorporated the French settlements of Louisiana,—the clergy and seigniors resolved to resist every assault of the Anglo-Americans, and to retain our country for monarchic Britain, 3,000 miles distant; a patroness all the less likely, for that remoteness, to become perilously inimical to Canadian institutions.

Besides, even had the Canadians not been outraged by the declaration of Congress against catholicism and French jurisprudence, they ever preserved in their hearts that hatred for the British race, wherever born or located, which they had contracted during long wars; they thus made no distinction, in their minds, between those of it mingled with themselves, in Canada, and men of kindred blood dwelling beyond: viewing both alike as one body of turbulent and ambitious oppressors. Knowing this common feeling, the governor might and did rely on a majority of the population following the lead of the superior classes in rejecting American invitations to revolt; his own popularity, also, counting for something in the matter. Upon the whole, then, his least favorable expectation was, that if the Canadians would not take up arms for Britain, neither would they fight against her. Several seigniors, on the other hand, promised to Carleton that they would march against the rebels at the head of their tenants. The sequel proved, however, that they undertook to do more than they were able to realize, for, when they did assemble their tenants and explain to them the questions at issue, with an intimation added, that the government looked to the Canadians for warlike support, the latter refused to fight the Americans: these 'neuters', as they were called, observing, 'We know neither the cause nor the likely result of the differences between the contending parties. We shall manifest our loyalty to the government we live under by a quiet and submissive life, but we will take no side in present quarrels.' In certain districts, some ardent youthful seigniors, trying the effect of menaces to constrain tenants to follow their lead, were obliged themselves to flee precipitately. . . .

On the first report of invasion, Carleton directed troops to Lake Champlain. There were but 800 regulars in all at his disposition. The people of the lower districts, indifferent to events, remained in their parishes; those of the upper districts, being nearer to the scene of action, were diversely affected; some inclining to side with the invaders, but, in general, from motives expressed . . . resolved to stand neuter. As for the Anglo-Canadians, who weighed so heavily in the balance when the agents of the mother country were disturbing her favors: they now counted for little, their numbers being so few: besides, most of those few were, openly or secretly, partisans of the Congress, and the governor was well aware of the secret meetings these held at Quebec and Montreal. Such was the state of things when martial law was proclaimed, June 9; the government having called out the militia previously, to repel invasion and maintain order in the province. This double measure, new to Canada, did not work well. . . . By prejudicing opinions, and recourse to threats, the indifferent were alarmed, and those who wavered were forced into open enmity to the government. The latter now called the clergy in aid. The bishop of Quebec addressed an encyclical letter to his flock, exhorting the faithful to be true to British allegiance, and to repel the American invaders. He strove to prove, at the same time, that their religion would not be respected by puritans and independents if these obtained the mastery in the struggle going on, and that it would be folly to join them. These sentiments were more widely developed by him afterwards, in a lengthy pastoral letter published next year. Meantime, neither the proclamation nor the encyclical, was able to move the Canadians from their stated apathy. . . .

Thus did the frontier contest [*south of Montreal*], through the partisanship of some Gallo-Canadians, take the color of a civil war. Most of the British in Canada, also, became during the autumn, openly or secretly, favorable to the American cause; while many among the rural populations near the seat of war either joined the insurgents, or prayed they might be successful; while the rest remained quite neuter. Only the clergy and seigniors, with a portion of the men in towns, stood up firmly for the reigning power, and their influence finally induced a majority of the Canadians to observe neutrality at least. It may be fairly assumed, then, that to the clergy of Canada, at this juncture, was Britain indebted for the conservation of the dependency now her greatest colony. . . .

[*After retreating to Quebec on November 13, Governor Guy Carleton*] found most of the citizens of the capital divided into two antagonistic camps, while a third party was undecided which standard to join. . . . The governor ordained, on the 22nd day of November, that all those who would not take up arms for the common defense should quit the city. A number of British merchants, Adam Lymburner at their head, retired into the island of Orleans, to Charlesbourg, or to other places where they had villas, to await the result [*of the siege*], and hail it with a cry of *God save the King!* or *The Congress for ever!!* according to circumstances. . . .

The Canadians, too, who had lost their all through accepting inconvertible paper-money for supplying state-wants, refused to receive the promissory notes of the American congress in exchange for their services or the commodities they offered to sell. In a short time, likewise, those country people who had been most zealous in the cause of provincial independence, began to cool on the subject. The greater number of the people, in fact, knew nothing of the over-forward proceedings of two traders in Montreal, named Price and Walker, who undertook in their name, to deal with Congress, as republican representatives of the colony.

Again, the Canadians who joined the American ranks, or who favored the pretentions of Congress, began to perceive that they would have to play a secondary, even a subservient part, as the struggle against British domination progressed. The Americans now among them to begin with, decided everything without consulting the inhabitants; they nominated officials, convoked public meetings, etc., without asking Canadian consent upon any occasion. Presently, the more thinking of the Canadian republicans began to regret that they had been helpful to let loose upon their country a band of armed adventurers, at whose mercy they were, without any proper means of repressing their excesses. . . . The prudence of General Montgomery much contributed, so long as he lived, to prevent an explosion of hostile feeling against his people by the Canadians, who began to express an opinion, between man and man, that it were better to obey one's own chief, under whatever form of general government, than to be indebted for political freedom to aliens (in all senses of that word). . . .

Persons are not wanting who, at the present time, reproach the clergy, seigniors, and burgesses of that day for a policy denounced as being yet more improvident than selfish. They regret that unjust prejudices should have become means for depriving their compatriots of a tempting opportunity for obtaining independence and freedom, perhaps without shedding a drop of blood; as, had the British been once expelled from the country, they never would have re-entered it. . . . In place of this liberty, thus rejected, what did they or we obtain? '. . . During this long period of political servitude [*1774-1840*] unjust treatment, and humiliation, the *personnel* of the executive has always been alien and hostile to the Canadians.'

To these animadversions it is replied, with sound reasoning, that it would have been injudicious to take part with insurgent populations which were anything but sure of being able to gain their cause; that, notwithstanding all their promises, it were imprudent for a community of catholics, of French origin, to throw itself into the arms of a confederation of provincials mostly of British race and nearly all protestants; . . . That to cut the matter short, prudential considerations, as well as loyal feeling, founded on the rational basis of gratitude for royal grace, bound our forefathers to adhere to the prince (whose domination had been indeed imposed upon them), rather than run the risk of faring worse as a member of an Anglo-American republic . . . for, after all, there were worse conditions than that of living under the supremacy of a European monarchy, powerful to protect.*

2 J. G. BOURINOT (1888-1901)
THE QUEBEC ACT AND CARLETON

J. G. Bourinot was a Nova Scotian Anglophile, who, when considering the question of why Quebec did not join the Revolution, refused to permit facts to dislodge any of his deep-rooted anti-American prejudices. It was Bourinot's contention that the Quebec Act was a magnificent piece of legislation that reconciled all French Canadians to British rule. Such was the efficacy of the Quebec Act that,

. . . Whilst the American war of independence was in progress, the French Canadian people remained faithful to their allegiance, and resisted all the efforts of the Americans to induce them to revolt against England.†

However, as far as Bourinot was concerned, the Quebec Act was not alone responsible for saving Quebec from the "dastardly Americans." Sir Guy Carleton's military skill added considerable strength to the Quebec Act barrier.

. . . If Canada was saved to England during the American Revolution it was not on account of the energy and foresight shown by the king and his ministers in providing adequately for its defence, but mainly through the coolness and excellent judgment displayed by Governor Carleton. . . .

---

* A. Bell, *History of Canada From the Time of its Discovery till The Union Year 1840-41: Translated From "L'Histoire du Canada" of F. X. Garneau, Esq.* (Montreal: J. Lovell, 1862), II, pp. 127-128, 131, 133, 136-137, 140, 149-150.

† J. G. Bourinot, *A Manual of the Constitutional History of Canada* (Montreal: Dawson Bros., 1888), p. 17.

When Montgomery and Arnold united their forces before Quebec, the whole of Canada, from Lake Champlain to Montreal, and from that town to the walls of the old capital, was under the control of the continental troops. Despite the great disadvantages under which he laboured, Carleton was able to perfect his defences of the city, which he determined to hold until reinforcements should arrive in the spring from England. . . .

Carleton saved Quebec at this critical hour. . . . Carleton certainly brought Canada securely through one of the most critical epochs of her history.*

3 W. KINGSFORD (1892-93)

CARLETON AND BRITISH IMPERIAL POWER

William Kingsford's ten volume History of Canada *has been described as "the classic formulation of the imperial interpretation of Canadian history."† For Kingsford, the American Revolution was unfortunate and avoidable. He was convinced that Quebec acted wisely in not becoming part of the American Republic, for because of the British connection, British North America would share "the greatness and glory of Great Britain" and would be "in the van of civilization."††*

Kingsford accurately described the lack of sympathy for the British cause displayed in 1775 and early 1776 by most French Canadians. Confronted by this fact, he was delighted to be able to emphasize the important role played by Carleton and the reality of British military power in finally driving out the revolutionary threat. In order to substantiate his questionable thesis, Kingsford completely distorted the essential nature of French-Canadian society before the Conquest. He was hopelessly inaccurate in arguing that under the Old Regime, which he considered to be autocratic and oppressive, the habitants *were virtual slaves of the seigneurs. He was as wrong in maintaining that British rule alone had been responsible for finally providing the French Canadians with "liberty," "political rights" and "prosperity." Kingsford's gross misconceptions regarding pre-Conquest New France help to explain why he was compelled to place so much emphasis on the French*

---

* J. G. Bourinot, *Canada Under British Rule 1760-1900* (Toronto: Copp, Clark Company Limited, 1901), pp. 67, 69, 70-71.

† J. K. McConica, "Kingsford and Whiggery in Canadian History," *Canadian Historical Review*, XL, no. 2 (June 1959), 109.

††Quoted in *ibid.*, p. 113.

Canadian's fear of a return, under the Quebec Act, to "the ancient system they had groaned under before the conquest."

. . . The only scrap of territory [*at the end of November 1775*] which remained under British rule was the city of Quebec within the ramparts. The troops of congress held the forts of Saint John's and Chambly: they were in possession of the city of Montreal, which had submitted to their authority, and Three Rivers had accepted the new rule. The country parishes were not in every respect satisfied, but any hostility which existed in those localities in no way gave ground for any serious anxiety. There was a strong loyalist party among the French Canadians, but the great body of them had given no aid in the defence of the country. South of the Saint Lawrence, the majority had taken part with Montgomery's troops, and in the neighbourhood of Montreal they had been indifferent and lukewarm even when service was accepted by them. The general feeling may be described, that, for the most part, they looked to see which was the stronger side. This was the more remarkable since there was a traditional hatred of the 'Bastonnois,' as the congress troops were called, and there was little doubt that every institution of the past was threatened by their success.

The fact is a curious commentary on the political cry so long the shibboleth of French Canadian political orthodoxy, '*notre langue, nos institutions, et nos lois.*' It is not heard so much nowadays, except from young and ambitious politicians desirous of flattering the prejudices of their countrymen, by the cant of extolling to the verge of folly what to-day would be found to be insupportable. Three quarters of a century back it was the accepted key-note of political fidelity. In 1775, it was the very dread of reverting to those institutions, of having again to submit to the arrogance and power of the *seigneurs*, and the exacting authority of a dominant church, which led so many French Canadians to accept the promises made by the invaders, of a future assured condition of liberty and freedom; the two words constantly prominent in the speech and writings of the advocates of the revolution. It may, however, be safely affirmed that there was never greater tyranny than that exercised by the majority who advocated independence. At no time, was mercy shewn to any one attached to the connection with the mother country. The number of those professing these opinions in the old provinces was still large, and earnest in feeling; but overpowered by the outrages of the mob, paralyzed from want of leaders, with no rallying point, without organized means of resistance, without strength to vindicate their opinions, they were subjected to unceasing persecution. There was no one to call out this latent strength, and no effort was made by the imperial government to aggregate and direct it. On the other side all was vigour and effort, while intimidation was incessantly exercised, and the political agitation was unremittingly persevered in. There was a constant appeal to the glaring wrong and injustice which the people were told they suffered, and artifice and violence were constantly practised to advance the cause of the revolution.

The French Canadians became dupes to this pretension. They had enjoyed British liberty for sixteen years, and had learned to treasure the political rights, which, for the first time in their history, they had possessed. There was no grievance of which they complained; they had become prosperous and comparatively rich. It was not resentment of any past injustice, but the fear of coming wrong which had arrayed them against the flag to which they owed allegiance. They had been made to believe that the government would revert to the ancient system they had groaned under before the conquest. What was strange still in the character of their hostility was, that the agitators who had called forth this disloyal feeling, by their constant misrepresentation as to the influence of the Quebec Act, were those who were prepared to sacrifice the French Canadians in every relation of life. It must never be forgotten, that they had demanded the legislature should be formed from the few hundred protestants bent on destroying the language, laws and religion of the new subjects, while the British government had unflinchingly acted on the principle, that it would be a gross injustice to consider the question in any other light than as one on which the great majority of the Canadians should themselves adjudicate. This paternal care of the new subject was primarily the wrong complained of by the English speaking inhabitants, and was the cause that many of them acted in open hostility. Notwithstanding this assumed grievance on their side, by cunning and misrepresentation they succeeded in leading many of the French Canadians to accept their view, that a wrong had been done to the province by the Quebec Act, of which the effect would be to throw the government, as of old, into the hands of the *seigneurs*, and that the *habitants* would themselves drift back to the oppressive times of *corvées,* compulsory service, and the harsh features of former days. . . .

That the few men who accompanied Montgomery were enabled to conquer Canada, with the exception of Quebec, and hold the country for six months, would be inexplicable, but for the facts that I have given. There were only nine hundred regular troops, for the defence of the whole province. Among the English speaking population, there was a feeling of active sympathy with the cause of congress. The Canadian *habitants* generally were neutral, or favoured the invaders. There was a strong party among them loyal to British institutions as they had been established; especially the ecclesiastics, and the higher and professional classes. They possessed, however, but little influence.

It is simply a duty to record that this feeling passed rapidly away, and never again obtained activity. . . .

It was, indeed, fortunate for Canada, that a man of Carleton's genius was at the head of affairs. He saw the true key of the situation was the possession of Quebec. So long as there was hope that the then western part of Canada could be held, he remained at his post. It was only with difficulty he arrived at Quebec, to inspire with fortitude and decision the few who remained within its walls. . . . The possession of Quebec during the winter of 1775-1776, was to determine who was to be the future master of Canada. Held by the congress troops during the winter, under a soldier so distinguished and experienced as Montgomery, it is hard to tell what would have been the fate of the fortress, if attacked in the ensuing spring, by the reinforcements which arrived from England. . . .

So long as the British standard stood on the walls, he [*Carleton*] knew that that day would come; and hence his effort to live through the winter in irresistible strength, so that, when the earth in spring had renewed her youth, he could purge the province of its invaders, and restore the pre-eminence of Great Britain in all of its power.

. . . [*By the spring of 1776*] The great mass of the inhabitants, both of town and country, had awakened to the realities of their position as a conquered people. They felt the weight of this occupation by men from the southern colonies, who, although belonging to the same empire, were without true sympathy with them and had entered the province as invaders and enemies, to effect their own political purposes. The balance in the scale was now turned;

all that was required was some weighty impetus to give it a *momentum.* When, in a few weeks, that power was irresistibly exercised, the strength of the country acted with singular unanimity, animated by the one desire to sweep from the province the force in possession of it.*

4 V. COFFIN (1896)

AMERICAN ALIENATION OF CANADIAN SYMPATHIZERS

Professor Victor Coffin of the University of Wisconsin attacked the views put forward by Bourinot and Kingsford. Coffin felt that the Quebec Act had disgusted most French-Canadian habitants *and had transformed them into potential revolutionaries. These people, therefore, welcomed the American invaders with open arms—but not for long. For the Americans quickly alienated their French-Canadian supporters. It was American "mismanagement" and not the Quebec Act or Carleton, that kept Quebec British. In addition, it was Coffin's contention that Garneau, Bourinot and Kingsford were wrong in arguing that most of the English-speaking inhabitants were sympathetic to the invaders.*

. . . far from being effectual in keeping the mass of the Canadians loyal to the British connection, [*the Quebec Act*] had a strong influence in precisely the opposite direction. The Canadians were *not* kept loyal, and Canada was preserved at this crisis to the British Empire through the vigor and ability of its British defenders, and through the mismanagement of their cause on the part of the revolutionists.

. . . [*in 1775*] there can be no doubt that the great body of the English were decidedly opposed to the step [*sending delegates to Congress*] on general grounds, and that the leading American element found itself at this point finally separated from its former constituency. We find in short that the main body of the 'old subjects' remained, in spite of the Quebec Act, heartily loyal to English rule during this crisis.

. . . But my main purpose in this chapter is to enquire into the results of the Quebec Act on the French Canadians. The generally accepted view that they were fully satisfied with the Act and

---

* W. Kingsford, *History of Canada* (Toronto: Rowsell and Hutchinson, 1892), V, pp. 483-486, 488, 489; W. Kingsford, *History of Canada* (Toronto: Rowsell and Hutchinson, 1893), VI, p. 45.

thereby strongly attached to the British connection, is one which, without examination of evidence, proceeds naturally from the belief that the measure was based wholly or mainly upon their expressed desires. . . . This was not the case, for the reason that the self-constituted interpreters of these desires had drawn their conclusions from very narrow and mistaken observation and very one-sided information. It is not surprising therefore to find that the results did not at all correspond with the expectations of the promoters of the measure. Overwhelming evidence shows that the French Canadians were not faithful to British rule at this crisis, and that they were least faithful at the time when the Quebec Act might be supposed to have had most influence. Further evidence, equally strong, if not so great in quantity, shows that the effect of the Act on the mass of the people was one of alienation rather than conciliation. . . .

It is very evident not only that the Canadians had overwhelmingly declared in favor of the invaders from the first down till the disaster at Quebec, but that even after that event a considerable number clung to the colonial cause and were still ready at any moment to attach themselves to any enterprise of vigor sufficient to give any promise of success. The ordinary judgment with regard to their conduct both from the British who saw in their neutrality even only the basest ingratitude, and from the Americans who experienced a very considerable change in the later months of disaster, is not sufficient or satisfactory. According to this, the people were moved mainly by fear and the desire of being on the stronger side; they embraced or acquiesced in that cause which was for the moment locally predominent. But to say that the Canadians were a timid race is to disregard wholly the facts of their military origin and training, and especially the strong testimony from both sides to their valor and conduct under the most disheartening circumstances in the last war. Nor is it sufficient to say that they had no interest in, as no knowledge of, the present colonial quarrel; that they had been growing prosperous, had devoted themselves wholly to the repairing of the ravages of the old struggle, and were now anxious only to be left in peace. The inevitable result of such a temper would have been the offering to the invader of their peace, if not active opposition, at least a stolid and hostile indifference; from which, as we have seen, their real conduct could not have been further removed. And this furthermore, takes no account of the strong influences that were brought to bear on the people from the British side. The chief of these were the strenuous measures resorted to by the clergy. Admitting all I have said as to the decreasing command of the popular mind by the church, it must still be admitted that for an *indifferent* community, the extreme step of refusing absolution to any one who had joined the invaders, might be supposed to have been a most powerful deterrent. Yet we are told that every priest in the country except one had taken this course. That the step was entirely without efficacy can not be supposed; no doubt it did much to prevent a more open and general rising. That *any* defection occurred in the face of it must be taken as the strongest proof that the Canadians were neither timid nor indifferent, but that they conceived themselves to have strong ground for discontent and apprehension. Their national feeling was not yet involved, for there was as yet no open connection between the revolution and France. In the entire absence of evidence of the existence before the Quebec Act of such discontent or apprehension as would now explain their conduct, we are driven for that explanation to the Act itself. It seems not too much to say that, supplemented as it was by the misrepresentation of its opponents, and still more by the most ill-advised attempt to establish through it the old military position of the noblesse, it drove the people into the arms of the revolutionists.

But it is further necessary to show that the defection of the Canadians at this crisis was not the momentary effect of sudden panic or of a passing wave of popular feeling. Active misrepresentation might go far to explain such; though only on the hypothesis that the English agitators and the colonial emissaries had suddenly acquired an influence very much greater than the natural leaders of the people. The Quebec Act went into force May 1, 1775, and was superseded on the following June 9 by a condition of martial law that continued about eighteen months; consequently before 1777 the people were not in a position to judge of or be influenced by it except as a matter of speculation. But misrepresentation as to it ought certainly to have been dispelled long before that time; from the spring of 1775 the government was in a position to do the worst that could have been apprehended. Nevertheless we find still in existence throughout the war a strong popular leaning toward the continental cause. There was of course no occasion or opportunity for open demonstrations; we must judge by the report of the provincial officials. The value of these is emphasized by the fact that the conclusions arrived at were not hastily formed or insufficiently grounded, but were the result of the most careful examination by the best methods available into the real sentiments of the *body of the people*, not as before of the few who had thrust themselves forward as their spokesmen. . . .

It must therefore be concluded that the Quebec Act had added no element of strength to the British cause in the Province; that on the contrary, while it had confirmed the allegiance of those whose allegiance needed no confirmation, it had been the main cause of the disaffection of those who otherwise would have been at least quiescent.

If the conclusion reached above be correct, we are confronted with a difficulty in the utter failure of the expedition. It might not unreasonably be concluded that such a failure bears strongly against the position I have taken; that if the Canadians were thus so favorably disposed toward the invaders, the utmost vigor and ability on the part of the few British defenders would have been wholly inadequate to the prevention of the definite attachment of the Province to the Revolutionary cause. To answer this objection it will be necessary to view the enterprise from the American side to see if any other factors enter into the situation. Such I think will be the case; it will be found that not only did the revolutionists fail to make any effective use of the Canadian alliance, but that by the mismanagement and misconduct of both officers and men, the Canadians were from the first impressed with the incapacity of their would-be emancipators, and were gradually driven by actual ill-treatment to neutrality if not to hostility. The favorable moment was let slip and did not return. With the spring of 1776 not only was the British force strengthened to a degree which enforced caution upon the most hostile of the peasantry, but by that time that peasantry had had its revolutionary fervour cooled by treatment as arbitrary and injurious as anything that could be expected from the dreaded revival of the conditions of the old régime. The evidence on this point leaves us wondering, not at the cooling off of the Canadians, but at the retention by them of any degree of respect for or sympathy with the revolutionary cause. That a very considerable degree was retained is shown above, and the fact testifies to the strength of the original feeling; but until the Franco-American alliance it did not again in all probability reach sufficient vigor to afford any likelihood of active manifestation.

It is not my intention to enter upon any full consideration of the invasion of Canada by the Revolutionary forces in 1775-6; full accounts already exist for all parts of this enterprise except for that Canadian side which it is here attempted to supply. The general causes assigned for the failure of the movement are well-known, and it is assumed that sufficient explanation thereof is given under the heads of such apparently unavoidable drawbacks as disease among the troops, short terms of enlistment, lack of ready money. Even if these difficulties had existed in the degree usually stated, it would be rash to assume that the responsibility of the authorities for the disaster is thereby much reduced. But the extent of these obstacles can be shown to have been greatly exaggerated. The degree of disease among the troops would have been found a comparatively small factor if disease alone had interfered with their efficiency; the lack of specie was at no time a fatal defect. It seems very evident that Congress never made efforts adequate to the degree of importance attached to the enterprise by leading military authorities. What that degree was is shown by many emphatic utterances. Washington, in his Instructions to Arnold, September 14, 1775, especially impresses upon him that the command is 'of the utmost importance to the interest and liberties of America,' and that upon it the safety of the whole continent may depend; further adjuring him solemnly to pay every regard to the attitude of the Canadians, 'bearing in mind that if they are averse to it, [i.e., the expedition], and will not cooperate, or at least willingly acquiesce, it must fail of success. In this case you are by no means to prosecute the attempt. The expense of the expedition and the disappointment are not to be put in competition with the dangerous consequences which may ensue from irritating them against us, and detaching them from that neutrality which they have adopted.' In the following October, R. H. Lee writes to Washington of the expedition: 'The ministerial dependence on Canada is so great that no object can be of greater importance to North America than to defeat them there. It appears to me that we must have that country with us this winter, cost what it may.' And four days later, Washington impresses upon Schuyler, who was about to lead the western part of the force, that 'The more I reflect upon the importance of your expedition, the greater is my concern lest it should sink under insuperable difficulties. I look upon the interests and salvation of our bleeding country, in a great degree to depend upon your success.' To Arnold in the following January he states that 'To whomsoever it [i.e., Quebec and in consequence Canada], belongs, in their favour probably will the balance turn. If it is in ours, success, I think, will most certainly crown our virtuous struggles; if it is in theirs, the contest at least will be doubtful, hazardous, and bloody.' That Congress shared in this opinion at a later stage at least is shown by a letter from the President to Gen. Thomas, May 24, 1776, in which it is stated that Canada is 'an object of the last importance to the welfare of the United Colonies. Should our troops retire before the Enemy and entirely evacuate that Province, it is not in human wisdom to foretell the consequences.' On the same day Congress forwarded to the Commissioners in Canada all the hard money it had been able to procure; sending in addition about three weeks later $20,000 in specie and $190,000 in paper. These funds might earlier have had an important effect that now was impossible; that the main obstacle was not now at least of a financial character may be seen from the statement to Congress by the Commissioners at Montreal, in May, that though there was plenty of wheat and flour in the country, 'it was with difficulty that either could be procured a few days ago, for ready money.' It cannot be questioned of course that the money problem was present from the first, and that it had an important bearing. The journals of the Arnold expedition show that however friendly the Canadians had been at the first contact, they were even then thriftily endeavoring to turn an honest penny from the necessities of the troops; insisting in some cases on the immediate payment of hard cash. But this dislike of paper money is easy to understand quite apart from any special distrust of the Americans, if we remember the ruinous experiences of the Province with it under the French régime, and the losses thus experienced since the war in spite of all the efforts of the English Government. However friendly in feeling, the Canadians were not anxious to run much risk either of person or property. But that they did risk something, and that the failure of ready money alone would not have seemed to them a fatal drawback, is very evident. The American force could not have existed in amity a month if the Canadians had not accepted promises, written and spoken, in lieu of hard cash; it was not until even these promises had failed and past ones had been disgracefully repudiated, that in combination with other matters, the financial element became serious. February 21, 1776, Wooster informs the President of Congress that he should soon, in the absence of specie, be forced to 'lay the country under contribution; there is no other alternative. We have not by us one half money enough to answer the pressing demands of the country people to whom we are indebted.' About a week later (March 4), Arnold issued a Proclamation giving paper money currency, 'declaring those enemies who refuse it.' 'Many [he says], received it willingly, but the greater part were averse to taking it.' The supply even of paper was however apparently soon exhausted, and we hear of the inhabitants being forced to accept receipts for services or supplies in the form of 'certificates not legible, with only one half a signature, and of consequence rejected by the Quarter-Master General.' The situation is probably accurately enough described by the Commissioners to Canada in their statement May 1st, that, 'The general apprehension that we shall be driven out of the Province as soon as the King's troops can arrive concurs with the frequent breaches of promises the inhabitants had experienced, in determining them to trust our people no further.' A week later they report that £14,000 is owed in the colony, and that with the payment of this and some ready money, together with a change in the ill-conduct of the expedition in other respects, 'it may be possible to regain the affections of the people, . . . in which case the currency of our paper money will, we think, follow as a certain consequence.' It is evident, therefore, that, in the opinion of those best qualified to judge, the absence of ready money was but a comparatively minor difficulty; that if the Canadians were otherwise well treated it would present no more difficulties than in the other Provinces.

To what ill treatment then had the Canadians otherwise been subjected? What misfortunes had they experienced from the American occupation, other than the lack of prompt payment for supplies voluntarily furnished? The evidence for the answer of this question is entirely sufficient, and undoubtedly shows that at least in the latter part of the expedition, they had been treated, not with the forbearance and tact so strongly recommended by Washington, not even as neutrals from whom nothing was to be expected, but rather, in spite of their abundant evidence of good will, as irreconcilable enemies.

One of the earliest explicit statements on this point that I find is contained in a letter from Col. Moses Hazen to Gen. Schuyler, April 1, 1776. After making some strong statements about the changed attitude of the Canadians, he proceeds to give reasons therefor: 'Their clergy have been neglected and sometimes ill-used; . . . the peasant[r]y in general have been ill-used; they have in some instances been dragooned, with the point of the bayonet, to furnish wood for the garrison at a lower rate than the current price;' half of the imperfect certificates given in payment being moreover later dishonored by the Quarter-Master General. Hazen encloses as evidence of his representations a letter from one Captain Goforth of the Continental force, commanding at Three Rivers, detailing outrages committed by the troops on their march to Quebec. 'A priest's house [Goforth writes], has been entered with great violence, and his watch plundered from him. At another house they ran in debt about 20sh. and because the man wanted to be paid, run him through the neck with a bayonet. Women and children have been terrified, and forced, with the point of the bayonet, to furnish horses for private soldiers without any prospect of pay.' That these complaints are accepted as just by Schuyler, or that he had abundant other evidence, is shown by his statement to Washington shortly after, that 'The licentiousness of our troops, both in Canada and in this quarter, is not easily to be described; nor have all my efforts been able to put a stop to those scandalous excesses.' He had previously expressed to Congress his apprehension 'that the imprudent conduct of our troops would create a disgust to our cause in Canada; it even hurts it in this colony.' These representations are thoroughly supported by the investigations of the Commissioners of Congress, whose statements as to the non-fulfillment of pecuniary obligations to the inhabitants have been already referred to. May 8th they write from Montreal that the Canadians 'have been provoked by the violences of our military, in exacting provisions and services from them without pay,—a conduct towards a people who suffered us to enter their country as friends that the most urgent necessity can scarce excuse, since it has contributed much to the changing their good dispositions toward us into enmity, and makes them wish our departure.' Congress did not need this report to be convinced of the truth of the charge, for we find it on April 23 resolving, 'That the Commissioners of Congress to Canada be desired to publish an address to the people of Canada, signifying that Congress has been informed of injuries offered by our people to some of them, expressing our resentment at such misconduct.' Matters, however, evidently did not improve; for May 10, 1776, Gen. Sullivan writes to Washington that 'the licentiousness of some of the troops that are gone on has been such that few of the inhabitants have escaped abuse either in their persons or property. . . . Court-martials are vain where officers connive at the depredations of the men.' In the following June Washington expresses his conviction that 'many of our misfortunes [in Canada] are to be attributed to a want of discipline and a proper regard to the conduct of the soldiery.' A few days later (June 21, 1776), an investigation was ordered by Congress. The report of the investigating committee on the following July 30, placed as the first of the causes of the failure the short terms of enlistment, which had made the men 'disorderly and disobedient to their officers,' and had precipitated the commanders 'into measures which their prudence might have postponed, could they have relied on a longer continuance of their troops in service.'

There would seem therefore abundant ground for the conclusion that the colonial forces had conducted themselves in such a manner as to expose to serious maltreatment even the most friendly portion of the Canadian people. The conviction will be strengthened by a glance at some evidence with regard to the general character and conduct of the rank and file of the troops; evidence which shows clearly that the invading force as a whole was, throughout the latter part of the expedition at least, afflicted with a degree of disorganization and disaffection fitted to deprive it of all claim to respect on the part of the Canadians, and to make misconduct inevitable. Very much allowance is of course to be made for the unavoidable defects that attach to a militia, and that were bound to be magnified in troops enlisted and serving under the conditions of the early part of the war. The fatal use of the short enlistment plan was something for which Congress was responsible; the lack of harmony and union as between troops of different colonies was certainly to be looked for. These features are found in all the early operations of the Continental troops, and the special difficulties and disasters of the Canadian expedition were sure to make them more manifest and injurious. But that in this expedition there was also displayed other and more serious and fundamental defects in the character and bearing of the men is hardly to be denied. The impartial observer is forced to the conclusion that the word mercenary would not on the whole be an unjust appellation. It will be remembered that the word occurs in the exceedingly strong language used by Washington himself at this time about the force under his command. He writes to Congress in the latter part of 1775 that 'Such a dearth of public spirit and such a want of virtue. . . . I never saw before; . . . . such a mercenary spirit pervades the whole [*force*] that I should not be at all surprised at any disaster that may happen.' And if this could be said of the troops assembling for defence in the heart of the country, we cannot be surprised to discover the same unsatisfactory condition in offensive operations of such magnitude and difficulty as those in Canada.

That the spirit in the Canadian expedition was unsatisfactory in the extreme from the beginning is shown clearly in Montgomery's statements. October 31, 1775, he writes: 'The New England troops are the worst stuff imaginable for soldiers. They are homesick; their regiments have melted away, and yet not a man dead of any distemper. There is such an equality among them, that the officers have no authority, and there are very few among them in whose spirit I have confidence. The privates are all generals, but not soldiers; and so jealous that it is impossible, though a man risk his person, to escape the imputation of jealousy.' The most strenuous efforts were found necessary to induce the troops to enter at all upon the enterprise; it seems most probable that, but for the general belief in the weakness of the enemy and the warm support of the French-Canadians, it would have been found impossible. The force steadily diminished; on the 20th of November, Schuyler writes to Congress that 'The most scandalous inattention to the public stores prevails in every part of the army. . . . The only attention that engrosses the minds of the soldiery is how to get home the soonest possible.' With this temper it was to be expected that the force would diminish even more rapidly under disaster. On the receipt of the news of the failure of Montgomery's attack on Quebec, Gen. Wooster writes to Schuyler from Montreal: 'Many of the troops insist upon going home, the times of enlistment being out. Some indeed have run away without a pass or Dismissal, expressly against orders. I have just been informed that a Capt. Pratt of the 2nd Battalion of Yorkers has led off his Company for St. Johns.'

There is some direct testimony as to the behaviour of the

troops at Quebec in the journals of survivors. In that of Henry we have under date December 12 an account of the sacking by the troops of the house of a prominent Canadian near the town, and the evil results on the soldiery. 'Though our Company was composed of freeholders, or the sons of such, bred at home under the strictures of religion and morality, yet when the reins of decorum were loosed, and the honourable feeling weakened, it became impossible to administer restraint. The person of a tory, or his property, became fair game, and this at the denunciation of a base domestic villain.' This writer indeed takes pains to assert expressly that only Tories were plundered, and that the peasantry were especially protected and respected; but the mass of adverse evidence forbids us to consider the statement of weight further than with regard to his own company. In Caleb Haskell's *Journal* we have a glimpse of the attitude of the time-expired troops. Under date Jan. 30-1, he tells how the writer's Company, 'looking upon ourselves as free men,' in that their time of enlistment had expired, were tried and punished by Court-Martial for disobedience to orders, and how, 'finding that arbitrary rule prevailed,' they had finally concluded to remain and serve (which they did until the beginning of May, decamping then at a critical moment). Some interesting particulars are further found in these journals of the conduct of those who were taken prisoners on the occasion of the assault. Ebenezer Wild tells us under date January 3-4, (i.e., on the third and fourth days of captivity), that Carleton having sent for a list of the names of the prisoners, especially of those who were old countrymen, 'they, [i.e., presumably, the old countrymen; in all probability meaning thereby those born in the British Islands], chiefly enlisted in the King's service.' More particular information is given by Capt. Simeon Thayer who says that the old countrymen were threatened by Carleton with being sent to England and tried as traitors. In the lists given by Thayer with regard to the American losses in the assault on Quebec, we find the following figures for all ranks:—killed, 35; wounded, 33; prisoners, 372; enlisted, 94.

We see therefore that fully 25 per cent of the prisoners at Quebec took service with their late enemies, apparently without much delay. If these comprised only 'old countrymen,' it is an interesting fact with regard to the composition of the troops. But we have little ground for confidence as to the firmness even of the acknowledged colonists. Col. J. Trumbull, (Acting Adjutant General with Gage), writes to his father, Governor Trumbull of Connecticut, on July 12, 1776, of encountering the remnants of the Canadian expedition 'ruined by sickness, fatigue, and desertion, and void of every idea of discipline or subordination.' Of the 10,000 men of the previous spring, 6,000 are left; of the other 4,000, 'the enemy has cost us perhaps one, sickness another thousand, and the others God alone knows in what manner they are disposed of. Among the few we have remaining, there is neither order, subordination, or harmony; the officers as well as men of one colony, insulting and quarreling with those of another.' About the same time Lt. Ebenezer Elmer says of the same troops, 'The whole of their conduct at Canada since the death of the gallant Montgomery seems nothing but a scene of confusion, cowardice, negligence and bad conduct.' In an account of the naval operations on Lake George in October, 1776, Trumbull further describes the dangerous influence exerted by Carleton over the prisoners then taken by him. These had all been allowed to return home on condition of not bearing arms again till they were exchanged; when encountered by Trumbull on the homeward march 'all [he says] were warm in their acknowledgment of the kindness with which they had been treated and which appeared to me to have made a very dangerous impression.' He therefore 'placed the boats containing the prisoners under the guns of a battery and gave orders that no one should be permitted to land, and no intercourse take place with the troops on shore until orders should be received from Gen. Gage.' When the situation had been presented to Gage the latter ordered that the troops should return home immediately without being allowed to land. This seems to show not only the ease with which the prisoners had been shaken in their patriotism, but also a very great lack of confidence in the main force. A glimpse of the genesis of these forces in the spring of 1776 is to be obtained from a letter of one Capt. James Osgood to the Chairman of the New Hampshire Committee of Safety. He informs him that he has enlisted for Canada about 60 good men; adding 'I have had a great number Deserted after paying them the Bounty and part of advance pay to support their families.'

I shall add but little on this general point. An account by an officer of the American force of the final withdrawal from Quebec seems to show that this closing act was by no means creditable; the writer describes it as a 'disgraceful retreat,' marked by the 'utmost precipitation;' he himself 'meeting the roads full of people, shamefully flying from an enemy that appeared by no means superior to our strength.' The commissioners to Canada write to Congress May 17, 1776: 'We want words to describe the confusion which prevails through every department relating to the army,' and point out 'the unfeeling flight and return at this juncture of all the soldiers and the greater part of the officers who were entitled to be discharged.' On May 27, after dwelling on the distressed condition of the army, they tell of the plundering of the baggage 'by those whose times were out, and have since left Canada. We are informed by Capt. Allen *that the men who, from pretended indisposition, had been exempted from doing duty, were the foremost in the flight, and carried off such burdens on their backs as hearty and stout men would labour under*.'

In view of these facts we must at least concur in the words of Washington, already quoted, 'I am convinced many of our misfortunes are to be attributed to a want of discipline and a proper regard to the conduct of the soldiery.' Nor can we demur from the belief expressed by the President of Congress that 'there has been very gross misconduct in the management of our affairs in Canada.' I am not interested here to point out that this misconduct on the part of the troops was supplemented by gross mismanagement on the part of the leaders, from Congress down; as stated before it is not my purpose to write a history of the expedition, or seek the full explanation of its failure. That purpose is rather to show that the revolutionary cause, as expressed in this movement, could in no sense attract the French-Canadians; that on the contrary, this contact with that cause must in every respect have acted strongly to repress the zeal of the ardent among them, to bring doubt to the most sanguine, to anger and antagonize not only the indifferent but even the amicably inclined. Herein is the explanation of the failure to secure for the movement that effective aid from the strong predilections of the Canadian people which had been confidently and justly expected. It is an explanation which is consistent with the existence of such a predilection in a high degree; in it I am confident, is comprised in the main the explanation of the non-inclusion of the Province of Quebec (and of consequence all Canada), in the regions destined to form the United States. It is, I think, not to be doubted that had the favorable attitude of the

Canadians been carefully cultivated, had the *personnel* of the invading force been of higher grade, had the means been furnished, both to enable that army to avoid all arbitrary conduct, and to avail itself more thoroughly of the French Canadian assistance, the campaign would have ended in an altogether different manner. Even if the disaster at Quebec had still been experienced, it would not have had the demoralizing effect it did have; the invaders would have been still strongly sustained by a friendly people until adequate reinforcements had arrived. It is useless to contend that the French Canadians were a timid race, and of little help to whatever cause they might embrace; students of the previous war find them in it, as throughout their whole history, displaying under the most discouraging circumstances, in very high degree the qualities of regular troops. It is inconceivable that in fifteen years they could have so degenerated. They embraced about 15,000 able-bodied men, practically all trained to arms; here was certainly a factor that, well managed, might indeed prove the decisive one. At the very least we are justified in concluding that with this aid organized and kept effective, the American force could have maintained itself in the country until the French alliance had formed a basis for more decisive operations. That alliance alone, when it did come, was sufficient to stir again to the depths the whole Canadian people, including even the classes which before had immovably supported the British cause; it is surely not too much to say that if the total withdrawal of the Continental forces had not enabled the British to get a firm control of the country, and to take all possible measures of precaution against new attacks or uprisings, the province would have presented a most favorable field of effort; a field the French would have been only too eager to occupy.*

By carefully selecting his evidence, Coffin tended to see strong pro-American feeling where other scholars would see only French-Canadian neutrality. He was quite wrong in declaring that it was "very evident . . . that the Canadians had overwhelmingly declared in favour of the invaders from the first." Furthermore, Coffin places far too much emphasis on the violently unfavourable

---

* V. Coffin, *The Province of Quebec and the Early American Revolution* (Madison: Bulletin of the University of Wisconsin, 1896), pp. iv, 485, 487-488, 504-507, 513-528.

reaction to the Quebec Act on the part of the habitants. *No account, unfortunately, is taken of their reaction to the Conquest and to British rule. It was not easy to be a happy conquered people.*

Coffin apparently failed to realize that supplying an invading force with food for a good price was not necessarily a clear indication of revolutionary sympathies. At the mercy of the invaders, most of the habitants *had no other choice. In addition, there was a widespread desire for the restoration of French sovereignty and some French Canadians naively felt that American occupation would be a step in that direction. But once American cash disappeared so did much of the sympathy of the French Canadians.*

Coffin also underestimated the importance of British naval power in making it virtually impossible for any American force to gain effective control of all of Quebec. Moreover, he significantly distorted the impact that the "disgraceful retreat" and "American plundering" had upon the sympathies of the habitants *for the revolutionary cause.*

C. TWENTIETH CENTURY VIEWS

It can be argued that only two Twentieth Century historians have put forward basically original theses to account for Quebec's refusal to join the American Revolution. These were Donald Creighton's influential The Commercial Empire of the St. Lawrence, 1760-1850 *(1937) and Stanley Ryerson's somewhat disappointing* The Founding of Canada Beginnings to 1815 *(1960). Creighton's volume places unusual stress upon geographic and economic determinism while Ryerson endeavours to fit Canadian history into the classic Marxist mould. While Creighton and Ryerson were plowing new ground, historians, such as R. Coupland (1925), A. L. Burt (1933), M. Trudel (1949) and G. Lanctôt (1941 and 1965), were refining and developing ideas first put forward in the Nineteenth Century. Two books published in 1966, Hilda Neatby's* Quebec The Revolutionary Age 1760-1791, *which contained a modern restatement of Burt's synthesis, and F. Ouellet's impressive* Histoire économique et sociale du Québec 1760-1850, *which significantly revised Creighton's approach, carried on the debate.*

1 REGINALD COUPLAND (1925)
ANTI-AMERICANISM AND BRITISH COLONIAL POLICY

In some important respects, Professor Reginald Coupland's work was a Twentieth Century version of J. G. Bourinot's. The British Conservative historian argued that it was "probable, in the highest degree, that, if the policy of the Quebec Act had not been adopted, Canada would have been lost to the British Empire in 1775, and no distinct Canadian nation could ever have come into being." Because he relied so heavily upon selected official British correspondence, Coupland failed to appreciate the profound disenchantment with the Quebec Act that existed among the* habitants *and he also refused to admit how sympathetic many of them actually were to the supposedly detested* Bastonnois. *It is interesting to note that Coffin and Coupland, even though they used the same sources, came to quite different conclusions concerning the impact of the Quebec Act.*

'How have we been deceived in the Canadians!' wrote Postmaster-General Finlay: and it was only natural that Carleton and his colleagues, their high hopes utterly disappointed in the first hour of trial, should regard the mere neutrality of the *habitants* as the basest ingratitude, and, ready in the moment of reaction to believe the worst of those they had once praised and championed before all the world, should ascribe it to nothing more manly or more complex than the cowardice of a people whose bravery they had tested in war and honoured in peace. 'As to my opinion of the Canadians,' wrote Carleton in 1776 to the Secretary of State, 'I think there is nothing to fear from them while they are in a state of prosperity, and nothing to hope for when in distress. I speak of the people at large: there are some among them who are guided by sentiments of honour, but the multitude is influenced only by hopes of gain or fear of punishment.' 'Your lordship will remember,' wrote Hey to the Lord Chancellor, 'how much has been said by us all of their loyalty, obedience and gratitude, of their habitual submission to Government . . . but time and accident have evinced that they were obedient only because they were afraid to be otherwise, and with that fear lost (by withdrawing the troops) is gone all the good disposition that we have so often avowed in their

---

* R. Coupland, *The Quebec Act A Study in Statesmanship* (Oxford: Oxford University Press, 1925), p. 194.

names and promised for them in ages to come.' 'Yet I am sometimes willing to think,' continued Hey, shrinking, as it were, from so sweeping a reversal of his old beliefs, 'that fear, joined with extreme ignorance and a credulity hardly to be supposed of a people, has been overmatched by the subtilty and assiduity of some colony agents who were very busy here last winter, and that they are not at bottom an ungenerous or disobedient people.' And presently Carleton, too, remembers the revolutionist propaganda and makes allowance for its influence. When the crisis is safely over, his views are the same cooler views he had held just before it came. He tells the Home Government in 1777 that the defection of the Canadians was only to be expected: they had been too much affected by seditious agitation to be 'suddenly restored' to their old subordination. And he recognizes now that the obligations of militia service and forced labour are 'a considerable burden upon the people and that, after the disuse of them for many years, it is not surprising they should forget the duty to which they were bound by the tenure of their lands and their original government.'

These second thoughts were fairer: for, all things considered —the decay of the seigniorial system; the simplicity of the *habitants*, their detachment from the outer world and their ignorance of the broader issues involved in the Revolution; the unconcealed disloyalty of a section of the British in the province; the lies, promises, and threats of the colonial agents; above all, the weakness of the British garrison and the invaders' swift and easy occupation of the country up to the walls of Quebec—there is little to be wondered at in the neutrality of the *habitants*. It might, indeed, seem almost more surprising that they did not take sides against their British rulers. Only some fifteen years ago, these Britons, who now stood on the defensive with their backs to the wall, had fought and conquered them. The traditional enemies of their race from the beginnings of Canadian history, they had won the day at last, torn down the flag of France from their old French citadels, cut them apart from their homeland, and set foreigners and heretics to rule them. And if many of the *habitants* by the end of that war had lost their ardour for the cause of France, there were deeper and more personal reasons for not loving their conquerors overmuch. Every war leaves its bitter memories and obstinate longings for revenge: and these British redcoats, so few and feeble now and cut off by the winter ice from succour or escape, were the people who, only some fifteen years ago, had killed their fathers and brothers, their lovers and husbands and sons. Stirred by such memories and by the pride of a hardy, fighting stock, the *habitants* must surely have been tempted, especially when the invasion was actually in being, to raise the old battle-cry and reverse the judgement of the Plains of Abraham. Had a few thousand of them joined the besiegers, Quebec must needs have fallen by assault. Had they risen *en masse*, armed only with weapons of the chase and the farm, they would have overwhelmed the meagre British forces by sheer weight of numbers and been strong enough in the hour of victory to dictate their own terms to their American allies.

Why, then, did they not seize their chance? Because, in the first place, to fight against the British Government was to fight for the colonies: and, though British soldiers had played the chief part in the conquest, the *Bastonnais* were older, more constant, more hated enemies than they. Threats came more naturally than fair promises from their opponents in the long, savage blood-feud of the border. 'An eye for an eye and a tooth for a tooth' had been the cry in those days: and the echo of it could not easily be stifled by these new professions of friendship and esteem. And indeed, when the ill-disciplined colonial troops entered their country, it could no longer be pretended that the old hostility was dead or the old 'low-minded infirmities' of religious prejudice blown entirely away by the breath of freedom. Washington had spared no pains to impress upon the leaders of the expedition the vital need of treating the Canadians as their friends and especially of avoiding any offense to their faith. Arnold, for instance, was instructed to punish with the utmost severity, even with death itself, any man 'so base and infamous' as to injure the Canadians in person or in property, and to punish also any man who ridiculed the Roman Catholic religion and its ceremonies or affronted its ministers. But, despite all precautions taken by the commanders, there were several cases of violence and insult. 'The peasantry in general,' confessed Colonel Hazen, 'has been ill-used.' Food, fuel, and the use of vehicles were sometimes forced from them at less than current prices at the bayonet's point. . . . Such a record may be favourably compared with that of many other invasions in history, but not with that of the only other the Canadians of 1775 had experienced: and there must have been many *habitants* who recalled the firm discipline, the considerate conduct, the full payment given for goods and services, in the days of the British conquest. And further resentment was aroused when the *habitants* discovered that the profits they were bent on making from the new-comers were by no means secure. The lack of specie figures as prominently as military insubordination in the story of the American Revolution as a whole; and nowhere was the colonial paper-money more distrusted than in Canada. Nor was there an adequate supply even of paper to meet the local costs of the expedition. It was estimated by the Congress commissioners in May 1776 that £14,000 was then owing in Canada.

But it was not only old causes for antipathy and new causes of resentment towards the *Bastonnais* that restrained the *habitants* from taking arms on their side. It was said at the time, it has been said since, that the policy pursued by British statesmen in Canada since the conquest, the policy which culminated in the Quebec Act, had made no impression or, if anything, a bad impression on their minds. But this judgement is only true of the Act itself in so far as it was misrepresented and misunderstood: and of the general policy which had led up to the Act it is not true at all. Uneducated and ill informed as they were, the *habitants* could not have failed to feel the general spirit of conciliation and tolerance pervading the new *régime*. They could appreciate with a plain man's simplicity certain tangible facts in their everyday life. They had expected ruin and oppression—and this is what those glib revolutionists foretold if they continued to endure the British yoke—but so far, at any rate, their fears had proved ungrounded. It was currently reported that Governor Murray and Governor Carleton had betrayed such a whole-hearted sympathy with their race and its traditions as to provoke the angry and open opposition of the British business people in the towns. They could see for themselves that their new master had not tampered with their faith. They could worship in their churches as freely as of old. Their priests were unmolested. Even their bishop was back in Quebec. . . .

But probably the strongest factor in restraining the *habitants* from joining the ranks of the invaders was the influence of their own kinsmen in the more educated classes. The *seigneurs*, it has been seen, no longer wielded their traditional authority; many of them were personally unpopular; and few, if any, of the *habitants* were ready to obey their call to military service. But it does not follow that every *seigneur* had lost all his influence with all his tenants: and at least the more elderly and more conservative-minded among them must have been deeply impressed by the unanimous and unwavering loyalty of their old leaders. All the records are agreed that the *seigneurs* as a body supported the Government throughout the war. Carleton's tribute in the hour of crisis to their 'zeal' and 'fidelity' has been quoted; and when in 1777 he drew up 'a list of the principal persons settled in the province who very zealously served the rebels in the winter 1775 and 1776,' he included only one Frenchman in it and he was a subject of Old France. The testimony of the invaders was the same. 'With respect to the better sort of people, both French and English,' wrote an American officer to his General, 'seven-eighths are Tories who would wish to see our throats cut.' 'As the introduction of French laws will make room for the Frenh gentry,' reported John Brown, 'they are very thick about the Governor.' The *seigneurs* are loyal to the Government, complained the Montreal Committee, because it respects their religion and offers them an equal share of office with the English. 'Of liberty or law they have not the least notion.' And with the *seigneurs* went a part at least of the professional and *bourgeois* class. But far more powerful than the influence of *seigneur* or lawyer or trader on the *habitant* was the influence of the priest. Social ascendancies and feudal ties might be weakened by time and conquest; but the Church, which in the infancy of the old French colony had been practically its ruler, had never lost its hold on the conscience of its people. The tragedy of Acadia had borne witness to the power of the priests in politics; and now among the Canadian peasants, close cousins of the Acadian, they laboured for the British Government with the same ardour and with the same spiritual weapons as they then had laboured for the French. For, while their immediate object had thus been reversed, their ultimate cause was the same—the cause of their Church and its faith. Their leaders were closely in touch with Carleton; they could not mistake the plain meaning of the Quebec Act; and they never doubted for a moment from which of the two warring parties to expect the greater need of tolerance and freedom. The bishop himself [*Briand*] was quick to give the lead. In May 1775, at the time of the first American inroad into Canada, he issued a *mandement* in the following terms:

> A troop of subjects in revolt against their lawful Sovereign, who is at the same time ours, have just made an irruption into this province, less in the hope of maintaining them-

> selves here than with a view of dragging you into their revolt or at least preventing you from opposing their pernicious design. The remarkable goodness and gentleness with which we have been governed by his very gracious Majesty, King George the Third, since the fortune of war subjected us to his rule; the recent favours with which he has loaded us, in restoring to us the use of our laws and the free exercise of our religion, and in letting us participate in all the privileges and advantages of British subjects, would no doubt be enough to excite your gratitude and zeal in support of the interests of the British Crown. But motives even more urgent must speak to your heart at the present moment. Your oaths, your religion, lay upon you the unavoidable duty of defending your country and your King with all the strength you possess.

For the rank and file of the clergy this was a clear, unequivocal lead. But indeed they did not require to be led. Had the village *curés* ever questioned the liberality and sincerity of the Government's religious policy, the confirmation of their tithes by the Quebec Act must have convinced them; and they knew from of old how very different was the temper and purpose of the militant Protestantism of New England. Congress itself, moreover, had gratuitously emphasized the contrast. In its Address to Quebec, while boldly confessing its antagonism to the *seigneurs*, it had tried indeed to cloak the religious quarrel with a phrase. But the Canadian priests had also read the Address by the same Congress to the British People; and, set beside its unrestrained abuse of Popery, the special pleading of the later document was instantly transparent. So gross and plain, in fact, was the discrepancy that effective use could be made of it to counter the American propaganda among the *habitants*: at one meeting, when a French translation of the earlier Address was read aloud, the audience cried out against the perfidy of Congress. It cannot, then, have been difficult for the priests to convince the *habitants* that on the question of their creed, at any rate, the *Bastonnais* were not their genuine friends, and that, even supposing that their British masters had proved themselves tyrants and persecutors as well as heretics, to escape from them by joining the Americans—unless indeed they could rise in such force as to hold their own against their allies—would be only to pass from the rule of King Log to the rule of King

Stork. Yet, argue and exhort and threaten as they might, they could not persuade their parishioners to fight for the British Government: all they could do was to persuade them not to fight against it.

From both sides, therefore, strong influences were brought to bear upon the *habitants*. Never before had they been exposed to such a gale of argument and counter-argument. Never had their quiet, uneventful lives been vexed by such conflicting appeals to their interests and their impulses. Small wonder, then, that, in the end, bewildered by the maze of contradictory assertions and desires, they withdrew, so to speak, into themselves and waited for the storm to pass. 'After all,' they told themselves, 'it is a domestic quarrel between Englishmen: it is not our business to interfere on either side.' Inevitably both sides were disappointed and angrily expressed their disappointment; for belligerents are rarely patient with the neutral standpoint in the heat of war. But in the event the neutrality of the *habitants* told in favour of the British. Carleton and his men could just save Canada without their help; their help given to the enemy, they must have lost it. And so, since the major part of the influences which told in favour of the British cause were directly or indirectly due to it, Carleton's policy had not proved in fact the failure that it seemed.*

2 A. L. BURT (1933)
THE BURT SYNTHESIS

Professor A. L. Burt's The Old Province of Quebec *was an unusually perceptive book which demolished many myths regarding Quebec after the Conquest. He followed Coffin in stressing that The Quebec Act was disliked by the* habitants *who were, therefore, at first, generally sympathetic to the American invaders. The* habitants

were not hewers of wood and drawers of water for their feudal superiors, nor were they abject slaves of the church. The voyage across the Atlantic had emancipated their ancestors, and for generations the freedom of the forest had been breathing a spirit of liberty into Canadian society. The habitant's attitude toward the seignior was also affected by subtle changes which the British Conquest had wrought in rural Canada.

* *Ibid.*, pp. 162-172.

. . . . The consequence was that the British régime saw the development of an unfortunate strain and stress in the working of the feudal system in the colony; the habitants were more than ever distrustful of their seigniors.*

However, in spite of both what he regarded as the sympathy of the habitants *towards the Revolution, and also Governor Carleton's many blunders, Burt had to explain why Quebec did not become the "Fourteenth Colony.' He found his answer in the weakness of the American military thrust against Quebec.*

The five month's siege of Quebec opened with the odds decidedly against the Americans. With the exception of their leader they were all amateur soldiers, and they were inferior in numbers, being only a thousand against at least fifteen hundred and possibly eighteen hundred. . . . Their artillery was little better than a few popguns would have been. . . .

A blockade was equally hopeless. Before the besiegers could starve Quebec into surrender, it was sure to be relieved by a British fleet, and their own term of service would expire. . . . The only advantages they possessed were a bold spirit and the friendship of the Canadians, two hundred of whom joined them in arms, and the second advantage was bound to decline as the invaders were forced to resort to paper money to procure necessities. The marvel is not that Quebec withstood the siege but that there was a siege at all. . . .

For three broad reasons quite beyond the control of any individual, the mass of the population turned against the Americans. The invaders were weak in numbers; their material resources had given out; and they were Protestants in a Roman Catholic land. In the early days of the invasion, the little loyalty of the Canadians to the British connection had ebbed and flowed with the apparent tide of victory. The capture of Ethan Allen, for example, temporarily swelled the numbers who rallied to support the governor in Montreal. Relatively few took up arms at all, but of these few, more were on the American than on the British side, and as a whole the Canadian people favored the invaders and assisted them in countless other ways, especially when they were overrunning the country. Then the big battalions from the south vanished and the Canadians saw that the Americans were not almighty. Their new-found

---

* A. L. Burt, *The Old Province of Quebec*, pp. 205-206. Copyright 1933 by the University of Minnesota, renewed 1961 by Alfred LeRoy Burt. University of Minnesota Press, Minneapolis.

friendship had been quite fortuitous, for there had been little or no mutual understanding, and it quickly dissolved when the habitants discovered that the invaders could not win salvation for them. They realized that the difference between revolution and rebellion was the difference between success and failure, and they wished to avoid the sad fate of rebels.

Equally powerful as a dissolvent was the way in which the Americans supported themselves. On first entering the country they had won golden opinions by paying for everything in good sound metal. When they spent all that they had brought, the Americans got more by borrowing in Montreal. The biggest lender was James Price, who advanced twenty thousand pounds. But these resources also gave out. Then the occupying army had nothing but paper for a people who had been sickened of paper only a few years before. As of old, the Canadians were reluctant to give their goods and their services for this stuff. But officers and men had to live and therefore they insisted, sometimes pointing their argument with a bayonet. Many a certificate was illegible or even without a signature, and sometimes kicks and curses took the place of the less offensive paper. More and more the weight of the occupying army ground down the peasantry. One cannot but pity these poor forlorn people.

A third factor was the influence of the clergy, which makes one wonder what might have happened if parliament, by adopting the board of trade's anti-Catholic scheme, had driven the clergy to throw all their weight into the American scale. But Britain had won them by the religious provisions of the Quebec Act, and the Philadelphia congress had alienated them by denouncing these provisions. In consequence they strained every effort to make their people loyal, even going to the extreme of withholding absolution from those who aided the invaders.*

3 DONALD CREIGHTON (1937)
THE COMMERCIAL EMPIRE OF THE ST. LAWRENCE

As far as Donald Creighton is concerned, the English-speaking merchants, attached in an almost mystical manner to the St. Lawrence River, were responsible for keeping Quebec British in 1775 and 1776. The French-Canadian inhabitants, on the other hand,

---

* *Ibid.*, pp. 224-225, 229-230.

were of little consequence to Creighton; they moved about aimlessly in the background as crucial decisions that would greatly affect them, were made by the commercial élite. In 1775 and 1776 the mighty St. Lawrence, somehow representing the British way of life in North America, was apparently threatened by the competing Hudson-Mohawk system which, to Creighton, represented the worst features of American Republicanism. He therefore grossly oversimplifies complex issues to make them fit a type of economic determinism.

*Creighton's analysis is a disconcerting mixture of penetrating observations and evidence carefully selected to fit a pre-conceived pattern, of brilliant sweeping generalizations and questionable pejorative phrases. Creighton does not in fact present convincing proof that the merchants played a crucial role in keeping Quebec British. He can not be accused of being unduly detached in his treatment of the merchants; on the contrary, he consistently seeks to justify or excuse their every action and attitude. His identification with this colourful group tends to sustain reader interest, but it tilts the balance in favour of the merchants. Moreover, by refusing to consider the French fact and by avoiding any serious discussion of the weakness of the American thrust into the St. Lawrence region, Creighton further weakens his analysis. In 1775 and 1776 the St. Lawrence merchants may have been fighting for "the north ern economy" against the "competing economy of the south," but it seems more likely that they were primarily interested in quick profits and were not concerned with such lofty theoretical considerations. Professor Hilda Neatby is more convincing when she maintains that the merchants "looked at provincial matters generally, if not exclusively, in terms of profit and loss—their own profit and loss."**

The Quebec Act and the American Revolution shaped the policy of the commercial class in Canada for the next decade. John Brown, the agent of the Boston committee of correspondence, met the merchants of Montreal on April 3, 1775; and on May 1 of the same year, the Quebec Act went into effect. The new constitution and the revolution, which entered Canada together, were in some important respects complementary in their results. The feudal and

* H. Neatby, *Quebec The Revolutionary Age 1760-1791* (Toronto: McClelland and Stewart, 1966), p. 56.

bureaucratic régime, legalized by the letter of the Quebec Act, was sanctified by the necessities of the war and the spirit of national defence. The merchants, their demands for reform answered with unending reiteration by the patriotic parrot-cry that the times were unsuitable for innovation, found it almost impossible to break Carleton's and Haldimand's illegally reactionary application of a reactionary constitution. Though they could not win their way to power in Quebec, the merchants could at least continue their efforts to defend the St. Lawrence as a competitive and independent economy in North America; and during the period of the American Revolution, there was as much need for this defence as there had ever been before. In the Quebec Act the British made public the abandonment of the scheme for the imperial control of the west; but, no sooner had they done so, than the Americans, irritated by this acknowledgement of the separateness and importance of the St. Lawrence, attempted to impose a second continental system of their own. They failed. The independence of the Thirteen Colonies was not the only conclusion of the revolution. Great Britain could not keep the whole of North America as a political unit dependent upon herself; but the Thirteen Colonies were equally incapable of making the whole of North America a political unit independent of Great Britain. The colonies gained their freedom from Europe; but the St. Lawrence kept its independence in America.

When, in the first spring days of 1775, John Brown talked with the merchants of Montreal, there was every reason to expect that they would accept his proposals with a savagely joyful alacrity. As Simon McTavish reported, they looked upon the Quebec Act 'with horror.' They stood aghast at the parliamentary enactment of what they had always considered the professional prejudices of their governors. They crowded into taverns and private houses at Montreal and Quebec for long and angry meetings; they appointed new corresponding committees, and in the autumn of 1774 petitioned kings, lords and commons. But the protests of 1774 against the Quebec Act were just as ineffective as the appeals of 1773 for an assembly. The merchants wavered in the accustomed manner between rage and self-pity. They were, as George Allsopp said later, 'wounded;' they agreed mournfully that they had been 'treated like step-children.' And at the same time, they detested and denounced Carleton as 'the first contriver & great promoter of this Evil.' The growing indignation of the past fifteen years reached a climax. And the impact of American propaganda and the advent of American liberators coincided nicely with it. Who would not have expected, what Carleton and the bureaucrats evidently feared, that the merchants would play their historic middle-class role, join with a peasantry oppressed by tithes and *corvées* and throw the province into the American Revolution?

As a group they could not and did not do it. There were individuals, of course, who went over to the American side and the group as a whole was resentful, moody and apathetic. But when the American solution was presented to them, they could not accept it eagerly and whole-heartedly. Their local protest could not be fused in a continental opposition and their dislike of the régime in Quebec could not grow into a desire for freedom from London. The character of the St. Lawrence system had formed and hardened. The economy of the north was moving, slowly, gropingly, but purposefully onwards towards its own separate fulfilment; and, in the main, it dictated the attitude of the merchants in this crisis. Union with the Americans would at once submerge the identity of Quebec in a general American federation and cut the vitally necessary economic relations with England; and these consequences were inimical to every interest of the northern commercial state. It was true, of course, that the continental association, by which the insurgent Americans had stopped all commercial intercourse with Great Britain, was an offensive measure which would not likely outlast the struggle that had given it birth; and, although Americans talked grandiloquently about the prospects of world trade, it was a certainty, foreseen by many on both sides of the Atlantic, that the commercial relations between Great Britain and her colonies would be resumed, even though their political relations were profoundly altered. But the Canadian merchants were reluctant to accept even for a moment the embargo which the Americans had adopted as a war-time measure. To break temporarily with a metropolis upon which they were vitally dependent, for the sake of colonies with which they were in constant competition, was completely unacceptable to the traders of the St. Lawrence. They had no desire to endanger their own commercial system, even for an interval. They wished to dominate in Quebec; but they were unwilling to cut the connection with London or to abandon their competition in North America.

The conduct of the Canadian traders from the conquest onward anticipated their attitude to American propaganda and the American invasion of 1775. The controversies in the Thirteen Colonies and in the province of Quebec pursued different courses through calms and crises of their own. The Stamp Act, which roused both the American merchants and the American populace, produced discussions and arguments in Canada which formed a mere feeble, irrelevant anticlimax to the stern struggle with Murray. The Quebec *Gazette* humbly suspended publication on the day the Stamp Act went into force. In the summer of 1766, when the paper was once more being issued, a man named Cawthorne, who was apparently a brief resident in the province, undertook to attack the Stamp Act in the pages of the *Gazette*. But another and irate correspondent denounced him as a man who wrote 'without the sanction or approbation of any number of the merchants of Quebec.' The Canadian traders delivered no petitions against the Stamp Act at either Quebec or London. In the autumn of 1766, when Sir Guy Carleton arrived in Canada, a majority of the merchants—seventy including French Canadians—proposed to include in their address of welcome to the new governor a prideful reference to their loyal acceptance of the Stamp Act. This address 'occasioned great disputes and very high words in the coffee house where it was left to be signed;' and a disgruntled minority of forty-six, including French Canadians, ventured with great daring to pen a second address in which this reference was pointedly omitted. After this little argument over the problems of imperial relations, which contrasted so oddly with the ferment on the Atlantic seaboard, the merchants settled down to business. In the late sixties and early seventies, political agitation in Quebec declined while it was renewed with greater intensity to the south. In 1773 and 1774, when the Canadians recommenced their political campaign, it was not in sympathetic response to the movement in the Thirteen Colonies but in direct reaction to the policy of the Quebec Act. The petitions which the mercantile minority sent to London in 1773 and 1774 were severely local in their subject matter; and until the Americans determined to spread propaganda in Quebec, there are few evidences of sympathetic communication between the two groups of colonists. It is true that Quebec sent a thousand bushels of wheat and Montreal a bill of exchange to the distressed patriots in Boston, in the autumn of 1774; but we have very little means of knowing how far these gifts were the result of really collective action of the merchants in either case. Jonas Clark Minot, who dispatched the present of wheat, was a native of Massachusetts, and not of sufficient political importance in Quebec to be included in either of the two committees of 1773 and 1774.

The link between Canada and the Thirteen Colonies was, to a large extent, a personal connection, maintained by a few American colonists in Quebec. It was strengthened at this time merely by a common sensation of embitterment, for the two societies had no real community of interests. In Canada this sullen resentment was almost entirely the effect of the Quebec Act. It was the new constitution which gave the Canadian merchants a momentary interest in the miseries and the new religions of the people to the south. If Carleton, as he was instructed to do, had relieved the archaic angularity of the Quebec Act by the modern ornamentations of habeas corpus, juries, and English commercial law, it is probable that the number of American sympathizers would have been still more insignificant than it actually was. Five years later George Allsopp argued awkwardly but not unconvincingly 'that if Governor Carleton . . . in the spring of 1775, had immediately convened the Legislative Council, and that they had as expeditiously passed such Laws as are held out in the said Additional Instructions . . . at a time when the minds of His Majesty's British Subjects were disquieted and it may be said the affections of many of them alienated . . . it is very probable, nay almost certain, that very few of the ill effects that have since been unhappily felt, would have resulted in this province, from the attempts of the rebellious colonies against it.'

It was in this state of disillusionment, resentment and despair that John Brown found the Canadian merchants. He presented the American proposals. Their objective was, of course, not the conquest of Canada, but the liberation of insurgent Canadian democracy. As their addresses, manifestoes, and congressional instructions clearly show, they hoped to persuade Canada to copy the accepted revolutionary procedure of the Atlantic seaboard—to elect a provincial convention, to accede to the union and to dispatch delegates to the continental congress. No doubt Brown presented this full programme; and Thomas Walker, who identified his province with himself and imagined both to be the victims of sadistic persecution, sponsored and supported him. But, when the merchants were faced with these concrete proposals, their anger seeped away with disappointing rapidity. In all probability they were profuse in polite expressions of sympathy; but they remained obstinately phlegmatic about direct action. Once more, as a hundred times before in the conflicts of the past, the necessities of the commercial state of Canada clashed with the demands of the Atlantic seaboard. To send delegates to the continental congress would involve Canada's acceptance of the non-importation agreements; and to cut the simple and essential tie with London would ruin the merchants and destroy their commercial state. In a lame and embarrassed letter the Montreal committee explained the difficulties to the Massachusetts committee to public safety. But John Brown was more blunt. 'There is no prospect of Canada sending Delegates to the Continental Congress,' he wrote flatly to the committee of correspondence in Boston. The St. Lawrence, the Shield and the commercial system based upon them separated the northern economy from the Atlantic seaboard; and neither a common embitterment nor a common ideology could really bridge the gap.

This was the real crisis. But, though the merchants had refused the American terms, they remained just as sullen and irritable as before. There was a mild revolutionary flurry on the day the Quebec Act went into force. In Montreal, some one decorated the bust of George III in the Place d'Armes with a chaplet of potatoes and an impolite inscription. One of the French-Canadian bureaucrats, Picottée de Bellestre, rumbled aloud concerning the atrocity of the deed and young David Salisbury Franks punched his eye for him. James Price travelled southwards as the 'informal representative' of the Canadian merchants at Philadelphia; but he was not, of course, an official delegate to the congress and the extent of his powers and the numbers who supported him in the venture are alike unknown. Letters passed to and fro across the border. There was much assiduous hunting of traitors on the part of the government; and Hertel de Rouville, another member of the 'aristocracy' who had an itch to become a bureaucrat, made himself painfully conspicuous as a detective. The sense of deep injury remained among the merchants and with it a confused, angry desire for retaliation.

But, though the Americans had left a way open, they could not take it. As a group they could not begin the revolution in

Canada nor could they commit themselves whole-heartedly to the American cause. The year 1775 did not witness the fraternization of two societies; it witnessed the invasion of the northern economy by the competing economy of the south. There was little that was novel about the invasion; it moved on what were, for America, venerably traditional lines. It was a renewal, on the part of the Americans, of that old struggle between the St. Lawrence and the seaboard which before 1763 had been magnified by the ambitions of Great Britain and France. The ghosts of Frontenac and La Salle had been conjured up by British statesmen and Montreal merchants. The Quebec Act affirmed the old aloofness of the northern economy and shouted its old defiance to the continent. Down in the Thirteen Colonies, puritanical democrats spoke angrily of Canada's popery and despotism. New Englanders coveted its fisheries and New Yorkers resented the extension of its western boundaries. But out of the confusion of these different emotions emerged dominant the old fear of Canada as a base for armed attack. For what reason had the British protected and segregated this strange, alien, northern world of commerce and militarism, of red men and white, of popery and paganism, if it were not to strike from it, as the French had struck, and by the same old routes, against the rebellious colonies? It was these old jealousies and fears and not the novel religion of revolution which inspired the movement against Canada. In May, ten days after the Quebec Act went into operation, Ethan Allen, Benedict Arnold and the 'Green Mountain Boys' took Ticonderoga and Crown Point. In November, a larger American army (for congress had sanctioned the invasion of Canada) captured St. Johns; and a few days later it began to close around the practically defenceless Montreal.

During all these proceedings, the merchants played a role which was partly equivocal and certainly unheroic. Carleton and the bureaucrats, who had considered the merchants politically unimportant before the passing of the Quebec Act, adopted the convenient but highly illogical belief that they were responsible for the disaffection in the colony. The French Canadians, those brave fellows who, according to the governors, were instinct with the warlike valour of their ancestors, showed pugnacity mainly in their refusal to follow their 'natural leaders,' the *noblesse*. Lieutenant-Governor Cramahé, an old soldier like Carleton, told the merchant Macaulay in great heat 'that it was our damn'd committees that had thrown the province into its present state, and prevented the Canadians from taking arms.' This was a transparent excuse, for, as a Quebec correspondent remarked to Maseres, 'they must make somebody or other bear the blame of their *faithful Canadians*, as they used to call them." It was also an exaggeration. The merchants did not set any very shining example of loyalty to government; but, on the other hand, they did not leap forward to clasp the knees of their American liberators. When Allen first entered St. Johns in May, he was met only by a single Montreal merchant, Bindon, who had galloped south with the prosaic purpose of watching over a consignment of provisions valued at £200. In September, when the threat to Montreal became serious, the merchants formed a militia company to defend the Market Gate. Some thirty of them took part in the absurd little battle of September 25, when Ethan Allen was captured; and at least one merchant, Alexander Paterson, lost his life. Even after Carleton had abandoned Montreal, some of the merchants tried strenuously to bargain with the American general Montgomery for the surrender of the practically defenceless town.

But there were pro-Americans at Montreal; and at Quebec, on Carleton's invitation, a number of disaffected merchants, John McCord, Zachary Macaulay, Edward Antill and the Bondfields, marched out of the town just before the siege began. We have no right to say that all the merchants who viewed the Americans with sympathy, openly declared their profession of faith; but since the Americans at first swept all before them and since for a long time they held almost the whole of the settled part of the province, it is reasonable to argue that the active mercantile sympathizers were bold enough to declare themselves. The number of those who did so is quite small; and Carleton's list of twenty-nine persons, while probably incomplete, contains all the important and some insignificant traitors. These men, Walker, Welles, Price, Heywood, Antill, the Livingstons and the Bondfields, are distinguished from the bulk of the Canadian merchants in several important ways. The large majority of them were natives of the Thirteen Colonies. A considerable number were professional men, army contractors or wholesale dealers in provisions; and with the possible exception of Thomas Walker, there was not a single important fur-trading name in the whole group. In other words, it was the men whose business activities were least attuned to the distinctive commercial system of the north, who went over to the enemy.

On the other hand, a great many of the more energetic, the more notable, the more thoroughly Canadian of the merchants had nothing to do with the whole affair. Isaac Todd, the fur trader, dropped out from the Montreal committee early in April, 1775. Thomas and Joseph Frobisher, Alexander Henry, Peter Pond (both Americans), Paterson, Holmes, and Blondeau were hundreds of miles away in the prairie country. Simon McTavish passed through the invasion with his usual cheerful detachment and reached Michilimackinac in May of 1776 to tell its gaping inhabitants a satirical tale about 'the great matters transacted since last Summer in Canada.' It was, indeed, with a curiously uniform celerity that the fur traders either disappeared into the forest or faded into political obscurity during the difficult years of '75 and '76. Those who were most completely committed to the really Canadian commercial system which was based upon the fur trade could not assist an American invasion for the same reasons that they could not initiate a revolution themselves.

As early as John Brown's visit, one of these reasons was clearly evident: others appeared during the course of the invasion and the occupation. When the Americans closed in around the town, the citizens of supposedly 'radical' Montreal presumed to offer terms for the capitulation. Among these terms, which were signed by fur traders like Finlay and McGill as well as by rebels like John Blake, were included the unsympathetic demands that the town's inhabitants should not be forced to lodge American troops and that they should 'not be compelled, on any pretence whatever, to take up arms against the Mother Country. . . .' But the third article was even more illuminating, for it affirmed once more, in the face of the enemy, the deepest necessities of the commercial system of the St. Lawrence. 'That trade,' so ran the third article, 'in general, as well within the province as in the upper countries, and parts beyond the seas, shall be carried on as freely as heretofore, and passports shall be granted for that purpose.' Here, in the very presence of their victorious liberators, the committee of the citizens of Montreal made no request for self-government and made no suggestion of union with the Thirteen Colonies. The merchants stuck to their commercial system and their trade.

It was precisely these deepest necessities of the northern commercial state which the Americans could not grant. They could not accept the merchants of Canada frankly and unconditionally.

For back of the merchants as individuals was their collective commercial system; and their commercial system depended upon the close connection with London and unrestricted trade with the Indians in the far west. But the Americans were fighting the British and they distrusted and feared the western Indians and the western garrisons. General Lee ordered Wooster, who was commanding at Montreal, to 'suffer the Merch[an]ts of Montreal to send none of their woolen Cloths out of the Town;' and this stoppage of free trade in the west completed both the dislocation of the merchants' commercial system and the process of their disillusionment. Their commercial distress, and very significantly their commercial distress alone, moved them to address congress. In the only petition which was ever sent by any group in Canada to the so-called 'continental congress' at Philadelphia, the fur traders, with one of the Frobisher brothers at their head, petitioned for the reopening of the western trade. Their action was not without its irony. Congress had expected Canadian delegates and hoped for Canadian entrance into the union; but all it ever received from the northern commercial state was a polite request to take its heel off northern commerce. When the American commissioners, Chase, Carroll and Franklin, came up to Canada, they reopened the trade and began to issue passes in the spring of 1776. But it was then too late.

The fact is that neither the merchants nor their liberators could grant each other's demands or live up to each other's expectations. The Americans would have welcomed the town meetings and nocturnal cabals of which Carleton so much disapproved. The merchants met on February 5, 1776, to debate their petition against the restrictions of their western trade; but no provincial convention and no committees of correspondence arose from even the free soil of Montreal. The traders stood apart in an aloofness which could be modified only by embarrassed politeness and often hardened into positive hostility. As early as December, 1775, Montgomery was writing to the generalissimo Schuyler at Albany that 'we are not to expect a union with Canada, till we have a force in the country sufficient to ensure it against any attempts that may be made for its recovery.' In Montreal and the countryside the Americans, who had intended to masquerade as open-handed liberators, were forced to maintain their real role of suspicious tyrants. Wooster, who was in command at Montreal during the greater part of the American occupation, reported that the merchants were not disposed to assist him if they could avoid it. 'With respect to the better sort of people, both *French* and *English*,' wrote the traitor Moses Hazen, 'seven-eights are Tories, who would wish to see our throats cut, and perhaps would readily assist in doing it.'

Of this estrangement which had existed from the beginning and which became merely more evident with time, there exists a further and a better proof in the matter of finance. Beneath all the distresses of the invaders was an enfeebling poverty which paralysed their own efforts and antagonized their potential supporters. Money was the one thing which lay in the power of the merchants alone to contribute; but they refused to make loans, to discount bills or to accept paper. James Price, who loaned some twenty thousand pounds, was an exception and was very significantly regarded by the Americans as almost their sole resource. Although he touted assiduously for the Americans among his brother merchants, he admitted himself that he did not find any of the Montreal traders willing to lend. The financial stringency had its comic as well as its serious results. The three wise men from Philadelphia, Chase, the wealthy Carroll and the complacent Franklin, arrived at St. Johns to discover that their reception had been somewhat imperfectly rehearsed. The courier which they dispatched in royal style to Montreal to warn the waiting city of their arrival, was stopped at the ferry on the St. Lawrence for the sufficient reason that he had plenty of paper money but no hard cash. Not a carriage would have moved from Montreal to bring back 'the first civilized American' and the wealthiest citizen of the Thirteen Colonies, if a single Montreal sympathizer had not pityingly agreed to foot the bill. 'It is impossible,' wrote the commissioners to congress on their arrival in Montreal, 'to give you an idea of the lowness of the Continental credit here. . . .' They pledged the public, and their own private credit in vain; and Charles Carroll's sterling bills of exchange were hawked fruitlessly around the town for days.

As spring broke in 1776, the British fleet moved up the St. Lawrence, the American army drifted chaotically west and south, and the American commissioners decided it was time to go. There was a slight scurry in Montreal among those who had committed themselves too deeply for pardon, and Price, Heywood and Bindon were busy with preparations for departure. But the bulk of the merchants watched the Americans and their few sympathizers press southward without regret or perturbation. The northern fur-trading colony, with the military and naval power of Great Britain at its back, had maintained its old independence in the continent. The Americans, as time was to show, could beat the British on the Atlantic seaboard; but they could not hold the towns on the lower St. Lawrence, nor could they capture the western hinterland of the fur-trading state. The Indian administration, the fortified posts and the friendship of the tribes were the three political expressions of western commercialism which naturally fell under the control of the northern fur-trading state. The Americans set themselves in vain to break this formidable combination. They were weak politically in the west for they were weak commercially. It is true that on the outskirts of the northern economy they won some military successes. In 1779 George Rogers Clark captured the post at Vincennes and its commander, Lieutenant-Governor Hamilton. But, on the whole, the Americans made little impression on the west. They could effect the temporary possession of a fort, they could and did prolong the unsettlement of the region. But they could not make it really theirs, for they could not break the commercial and military supremacy of the northerners on the Great Lakes.*

4 GUSTAVE LANCTÔT (1941)

THE NEUTRAL FRENCH CANADIANS

It is Major Lanctôt's contention that even though some French Canadians were militant royalists and others just as militant supporters of the Revolution, the vast majority of French Canadians adopted a position of neutrality. They did so because of "self-interest," "prudence" and the desire for "self-preservation." Because of the widespread neutrality rather than enthusiastic and militant support for the Americans, there was really no hope that the Revolution would succeed in Quebec. Lanctôt's emphasis is somewhat original but his evidence is not; he also studiously avoids strategic considerations.

---

* Reprinted from *The Empire of the St. Lawrence* by D. G. Creighton by permission of the Author and the Macmillan Company of Canada Limited.

Finally, beside a loyalist minority and a minority in favour of Congress, the great majority of Canadians were anxious to remain neutral at any price. How is it possible to explain such an attitude after the Quebec Act? In the first place, being mainly a peasant population the Canadians hated warfare. Why should they give their lives for foreigners, who had been their enemies, when the British subjects in Canada were refusing to do the same? Furthermore the English merchants and 'colonists' had shown consummate skill in presenting the Quebec Act as an oppression of the colonial settlers by tithes, taxes and seignorial dues as well as by forced military service from which they could only gain exemption through Congress. Finally when 'some troops . . . would in all likelihood have prevented this general Defection' of the Canadians, the British could not succeed in getting together 600 soldiers, whereas the colonies were invading the country with a show of considerable manpower. Faced with this series of circumstances, the Canadians opted in favour of neutrality for motives of self-interest, prudence and 'self-preservation'. . . .

Montgomery's defeat made terrible inroads into American prestige revealing as it did so, that behind the facade and the motives of self-interest, there were very few real 'friends of America.' When the news was brought on January 17th, Congress ordered that reinforcements be sent and that a second regiment be raised in Canada. Then it sent another letter to the inhabitants of Quebec telling them that the colonies were to continue to give battle and simply asking them to send delegates to Congress.

This invitation had no effect. In spite of an attempt by Wooster in Montreal, the Canadians were not in favour of nominating twelve delegates, six English and six French. Then another attempt was made elsewhere. Since the priests withheld the sacraments from Canadian recruits, Arnold found a chaplain for the Livingstone regiment in the person of Father Louis de Lotbinière, a former friar of dubious reputation. In Montreal Hazen obtained for his new regiment the services of the Jesuit minister Floquet. In spite of the presence of army chaplains, in spite of the payment of wages plus extra incentives, recruitment progressed so slowly that the American army was never able to boast more than 500 Canadian volunteers, and most of these were well below average ability. Carleton, on the other hand, had raised an army of 2,000 by the previous autumn.

But the rebel cause found its staunchest supporters in the English merchants, either American or British. It was they who together with Price, Walker and Haywood, advised Arnold and Wooster, provided food and supplies, even rum and munitions and advanced the necessary funds to pay the occupying army. Because of their frequent trips throughout the country districts, these men were especially responsible for maintaining colonial prestige, propagating their democratic ideas and assuring the colonies of the good will and neutrality of the habitants. . . .

Under their influence, numerous parishes on the outskirts of Quebec were willing to place themselves at the disposal of the invaders, to perform fatigue-duty or supply wood, and even to build ladders or fascines. In several of these parishes, members of the militia stood guard duty for the Americans and organized a system of signals should an English fleet be sighted. In others, the pro-Americans robbed and pillaged, stopped or disarmed their Royalist fellow-citizens. A few women threw themselves into campaigning enthusiastically on behalf of the Americans. These latter were able to count particularly on several Canadian zealots who showed their true mettle, for, being admirable leaders, they proved to be as untiring in their efforts as they were energetic. Such were Clement Gosselin, Germain Dionne and Pierre Ayotte. With the exception of two notaries and one lawyer, these partisans were recruited from among those outside the ruling class who had remained faithful to the English cause. In the towns, the Canadian leaders of the Congressional movement were Frenchmen from France, like Du Calvet, Cazeau and Jantard in Montreal, and Christopher Pélissier in Trois-Rivières. Thanks to the American siege of Quebec those who were sympathetic to the American cause had the upper hand in the country and easily imposed their will on a population who were indeed happy to see its former conquerors in a state of oppression.

Although the country remained passive, a Royalist element of considerable strength existed. Arnold wrote of the Montrealers 'they are in general our bitter enemies.' Certain parishes refused categorically to assist the rebels or to break the neutrality, while, in many others, even in the suburbs of Quebec, the most ardent supporters of the Americans were either very closely watched or disarmed. But the best interests of the Royalists were served by the clergy. Apart from a few exceptions like the Jesuits Floquet and Huguet, Father de Lotbinière and Father La Valinière, the clerics, following the instructions of Bishop Briand, preached the gospel of fidelity to England. Those who ran counter to his precepts, he withheld the sacraments. In his imposition of this penalty he was inflexible. For such conduct he was roundly criticised, insulted and persecuted by the Canadians themselves. Having been denounced by their parishioners, several priests from the Montreal area, and at least five others from the Quebec district, were hauled up before American officers. Parishioners inveighed against the teachings of their priests and even went so far as to criticise the attitude of their Bishop. But, in spite of the protests, the directives of the clergy continued nevertheless to influence the majority of the populace. Moreover, the priests and the upper middle class, both being Royalist, presented the letters from Congress in an unfavourable light and with the support of the Tory newspapers in New York, asserted that the goal of the rebels was to deprive the Canadians of their religion and their wealth. Another thing which did considerable harm to a people who possessed a grasping peasant mentality, was that the American troops, short of cash, neglected to pay the recruits for their fatigue-duty and even for their supplies. They were paid with valuless receipts or worthless paper money. Since the people had been robbed on a previous occasion by the use of French paper money, they refused to accept those bills issued by Congress in spite of Arnold's proclamation. Furthermore the American forces showed their inability to capture Quebec. Disregarding orders, companies of American soldiers set out for the colonies as soon as their enlistment period was over. Those that returned as reinforcements proved to be no more than an insignificant handful and smallpox wreaked havoc amongst the troops. Finally, driven to extremes by their failure, the Americans lost all control; they manhandled the priests, forced the peasants, at gun point to hand over food supplies and in certain cases even pillaged their houses. The Canadian 'Congressionalists' also drew attention to their behaviour by the terrible treatment that they meted out and by their pillaging of the homes of their Royalist fellow-citizens.

In these circumstances the majority, 'fond of [belonging to] the strongest party' kept their eyes glued seawards telling themselves that the English fleet would bring about a final decision, just as they had done in 1760: this attitude caused Wooster to remark that: 'there is but little confidence to be placed in the Canadians. . . .'

When English supremacy was reestablished, many Canadians joined the Royalist army. Some fought at Cedres, others at Trois-Rivières, still others formed the vanguard of the army that marched on Saint-John, so that Carleton thanked them for their services. 'The Great Joy expressed by the inhabitants on our informing them what a large body of troops we had coming to their relief is not to be described after all they had suffered during the winter.' On the whole, the outlook of the province was unchanged. 'The clergy and better class of people are strongly attached to government; as to the body of the inhabitants, they seemed to wish to remain neuter, or at any rate to join with the strongest side. . . . They appeared to afford us every assistance.' Realising the advantages of living in tranquility under a just government, 'all the parishes appeared quite rightly to have regained their reason, at least in the case of the majority of their inhabitants.' As for the minority who had compromised themselves in different degrees by supporting the enemy, Carleton formed two commissions with the responsibility of conducting an inquiry into their behaviour. The resulting information revealed that in the majority of cases there was a strong leaning towards neutrality. Most important, this inquiry revealed the presence of a pro-rebel minority group who, avid in their support of American troops, had taken charge of the parishes, terrorising the Royalists and forcing them, by threats, by their desire for profit, or by simple passive resistance, to provide supplies and assistance to the invaders. A still graver fact was that this minority opposed the clergy openly, denying them the right to intervene in the matter and going so far as to instigate the arrest of several priests. Finally the inquiry proved that a Royalist minority also existed, though more or less secretly, who though incapable of action, were nonetheless loyal to the cause and who drew widespread support from the clergy.

In the different parishes, the commissioners assembled the militia, severely reprimanded the turncoats, forced the officers themselves to burn the commissions they had received from the Americans and elected new officers who were given royal commissions.*

---

* G. Lanctôt, *Les Canadiens Français et leurs voisins du sud* (Montreal: Editions B. Valequette for Carnegie Endowment for International Peace, 1941), pp. 105-106, 109-113, 115-116, 123-124. Lanctôt has developed his thesis further in *Le Canada et la Révolution Américaine* (Montréal: Librairie Beauchemin, 1965). Translated for this edition by George A. Rawlyk.

5 MARCEL TRUDEL (1949) MONTGOMERY WAS NOT LAFAYETTE

Professor Trudel is of the opinion that most French Canadians were unwilling to support wholeheartedly the American invaders until it was absolutely certain that the Americans would be "les maîtres absolus du pays." *Until that time the* habitants *were content to be neutral. Trudel also raises the fascinating question—if Montgomery had been Lafayette would things have been different? Trudel's answer, though mere speculation, throws some penetrating light on how weak the British position actually was in Quebec during the Revolution. Moreover, Trudel suggests that the desire to restore French sovereignty was an issue of some consequence in Quebec in 1775 and 1776.*

If it were permissible for the historian, merely as an exercise in conjecture, to reconstruct the past in a setting other than that which really existed, then we would be confronted by the following question: if the invasion by Lafayette had been as carefully prepared and handled with at least the same dexterity as that of Montgomery in the autumn of 1775, what sort of reception would the Canadians have given him? We are aware that in 1775 and in 1776 the ruling classes in Canada had refused to become collaborators, either through a desire to remain faithful to their oath of allegiance, or to retain their legitimate attitude of defiance towards a traditional enemy; and that, on the whole the populace had remained neutral: but how would the Canadians have reacted to Lafayette? In 1778, the situation was no longer the same; while it may well be true to say that American prestige in Canada reached an all time low during the last months of the occupation, one might also say that the Canadians must have been sorely tempted to change their attitude towards the Americans. The Americans had declared their independence from the British Crown. As far as the Canadians were concerned, the hope of breaking away from England and of becoming a free nation, even though it might mean entering into a confederation with neighboring states, would certainly have presented a most attractive objective. Moreover, the leader of the invasion was neither American nor Protestant. He was a French Catholic belonging to the nobility of France and he was accompanied by quite a number of French officers. Lafayette's arrival was symbolic of the return of the *Fleur de Lys*. This symbol could well have fired the imaginations of the populace with memories of the brilliant exploits undertaken by Montcalm and Levis eighteen years earlier. Left to make their own choice, how would the Canadians have reacted? There is no doubt that Bishop Briand would have exacted from his people the same fidelity to their oath of allegiance; but on the whole, these people, while not having contravened their bishop's decree at the time of the American invasion, had none the less turned a deaf ear to his entreaties that they join Carleton's militia.

Neutral in 1775 through either reluctance or apathy, how would these people have reacted to Lafayette? But all this forms part of a history that never really was and which we must categorise under the heading of sheer fantasy.*

6 STANLEY RYERSON (1960)
A MARXIST INTERPRETATION

Is Marxism relevant to Canadian history? Ryerson vigorously maintains that it is and attempts to use a Marxist interpretation to explain the failure of the Revolution in Quebec. After reading his account of events in Quebec during the years 1775 and 1776, one is almost forced to conclude that a Marxist interpretation may be relevant; Ryerson's is not, however, since he has failed to apply the Marxist framework in a convincing manner. Nevertheless, Ryerson does put his finger on one important fact when he observes that the Declaration of Independence occurred after the American invasion and withdrawal from Quebec. Some other historians have failed to take into account this significant point. Prior to the Declaration, Washington's officers were still raising their glasses to George III in their mess. It is unfortunate that Ryerson fails to develop his argument concerning the effects of the delay in declaring independence on the failure of the Revolution in Quebec.

In April, 1775, the gunfire at Lexington and Concord signalled the outbreak of the revolutionary war. In his 'Letter to American Workers' (1918) V. I. Lenin wrote: 'The history of contemporary, civilized America opens with one of those great truly liberat-

---

* M. Trudel, *Louis XVI, Le Congrès Américain et le Canada 1774-1789* (Quebec: Laval University Press, 1949), pp. 108-109. Translated for this edition by George A. Rawlyk.

ing, truly revolutionary wars, of which there have been so few among the vast number of wars of plunder caused, like the present imperialist war, by squabbles among kings, land-owners, capitalists, over the partition of captured lands or plundered profits. That was a war of the American people against English pillagers who oppressed and held America in colonial enslavement. . . .' Almost from the start, Canada was involved. Spurred by the need to obtain arms, a border force led by Ethan Allen and Benedict Arnold on May 10 took Ticonderoga in a surprise attack and moved briefly against St. John's. Congress at first was hesitant about authorizing an invasion of Canada: but after the battle at Bunker Hill (June 17) it decided to go ahead. Noting that at Quebec was to be found 'the greatest store of munitions ever assembled in America,' George Washington argued that it would be 'folly not to do all possible to capture it.' Canada in British hands was too serious a threat to the rebelling colonies: a second Message to the Canadians emphasized that not they, but the British forces of occupation were the enemy.

The effectiveness of the Quebec Act was now put to the test. The clergy proved to be, as Carleton had intended, 'the most precious royalist agent.' In May, a month before the Governor declared martial law, the Bishop of Quebec issued a mandate promising papal indulgences for all who should take up arms against the American rebels, and threatening refusal of the sacrament and even excommunication for those who refused to do so. The seigneurs, for their part, set about acting as recruiting agents for the British authorities.

The masses of the Canadians reacted to all this in a manner that shocked and startled their rulers. Parish after parish—Berthier, Joliette, St. Michel, St. Thomas—protested against clerical intervention. The business of the bishop, declared one resolution, was 'to make priests:' this was a conflict that 'had nothing to do with religion.' Hatred of the church tithe, reimposed by the Quebec Act, lent an edge to the opposition: and the bishop's subsidy of £200 from London was lampooned in ribald ballads. The mass resentment displayed in this crisis was the first expression of an opposition to clerical interference in political matters that later became an important part of the democratic tradition of the French Canadian people.

The attempts of the seigneurs to recruit volunteers for the British service met with an even more vehement rebuff. Asked to raise a force of 6,000 men, Carleton could not muster 300. At Berthier a roadside meeting of habitants took an oath not to take arms against the American colonists, nor to fight 'to defend a pack of rascally pensioners of the Crown.' At Terrebonne they defied the seigneur; another seigneur fled to Montreal to escape the wrath of his tenants. In some instances the repeal of the Quebec Act was demanded as a condition of support to the authorities.

In many parishes the women carried on an active agitation. A British commission which conducted an investigation throughout the parishes after the American withdrawal included in its report items such as these:

'St. Pierre, Isle d'Orleans: . . . The wife of Augustin Chabot . . . going everywhere from house to house, perverted by her seditious speeches almost all the habitants; it appears that this woman has a most eloquent tongue and according to several persons made a profound impression on their minds.'

'Pointe-aux-Trembles: . . . The wives of Joseph and Jean Goulet went from door to door to blacken the names of those who last autumn urged the young fellows to march (with the British) . . . claiming that they were being led to the slaughter. . . .'

From Montreal troops had to be sent to restore 'order' in such 'indocile parishes' as St. Martin, Ste. Rose, Vaudreuil. The farmers of the Richelieu valley in particular were strong in their sympathies with the revolution: six parishes there, with a muster roll of 1500 men capable of bearing arms, repudiated all allegiance to the British Crown. The merchants at Montreal refused to enrol in the militia; at Quebec they held illegal 'town meetings.'

As Carleton saw it, the trouble with the Canadians was that they had 'imbibed' too freely of 'the American spirit of Licentiousness and Independence.' The feudal upper classes had shown themselves to be powerless. He was forced to appeal for large-scale help from London.

It was not until August that Congress gave its orders for a two-pronged move on Canada—via the well-trodden Richelieu route in the west and the ill-cleared, little known Kennebec-Chaudière trail in the east. Montgomery commanded the former, Arnold the latter operation.

Montgomery's advance on Montreal was held up for two months by the resistance of Carleton's main force of regulars at St. Johns. The capture of this fort by the Americans in November opened the gateway to Montreal. The inhabitants greeted the revolutionary army, declaring in an address that they accepted 'the union offered by our brothers of the colonies,' on the basis of 'the same laws and prerogatives, proportional contribution, sincere union and permanent peace.'

Carleton, escaping from Montreal just as the Americans were arriving, hastened downstream to organize the defense of Quebec. Arnold's men, after an exhausting trek through the bush, over a route never used by a large force, were laying seige to the town. They were soon joined by the force under Montgomery from Montreal. Cramahé, the Governor's deputy, reported that 'the Rebels being in Force, have upon their side the Canadian Peasants, whom neither the zealous exertions of the Gentry, Clergy or Bourgeoisie could prevail upon to do their duty.' Carleton moved to secure his position within the walls by expelling every one of 170 families suspected of sympathy with the rebels.

In the night of Dec. 31, under cover of a blizzard, the beseigers attempted to storm the Lower Town. The operation failed, and cost the life of Montgomery as well as of a large number of the attacking troops. Under Arnold, the siege continued, despite sickness, shortage of supplies and ammunition, until the spring. When, on May 6, a British fleet arrived with a powerful body of reinforcements under Gen. Burgoyne, the siege could be maintained no longer. Arnold withdrew his men to the Richelieu and thence southward.

The invasion of Canada had failed.

Militarily, one important cause of failure at Quebec was the lack of siege artillery and supplies for an operation conducted at a vast distance from the main base of operations in Massachusetts; another was British naval superiority, which forced the raising of the siege.

But the fundamental causes lay deeper.

True, there was widespread anti-feudal agitation and strong sympathy with the American revolt; yet something was lacking. No general uprising took place on the St. Lawrence. Quebec was far from being at the same advanced stage of social and economic development as the Atlantic colonies: capitalist manufacture scarcely existed there. The main issue on which the Canadians *might* have risen in alliance with the Americans was that of national independence from alien rule. But the American colonies themselves had not yet taken a stand for outright independence. Their Declaration of Independence was adopted only *after* the invasion of Canada had failed. 'If this declaration had been made nine months earlier,' ruefully commented the revolutionary democrat Samuel Adams, 'Canada would be ours today.'

The fact is that due to the influence of the ruling propertied classes in the colonies, the war was not yet being waged in a revolutionary way. Their hesitations were reflected in the failure to combine a political offensive with the military one. Commissioners sent by Congress in November 1775 to assure the Canadians that their religious and other rights would be safeguarded, and to organize the holding of elections in liberated territory, ventured no farther than Ticonderoga. Another, which included Benjamin Franklin, came to Montreal in May of '76; but its pledge that 'the government of everything relative to their religion and clergy shall be left entirely in the hands of the good people of the province'—was given only on the eve of the evacuation of Montreal, when Arnold was in full retreat from Quebec.

These weaknesses in the political conduct of the revolutionary war made it easier for the British and their clerical helpers to neutralize important sections of the population who, while ready to assist the American troops in various ways, were not prepared to join them in military operations. (At no time were more than 500 Canadians enrolled for service with Congress.) This attitude was reinforced by French Canadian distrust of the English merchants, among whom were some of the most active supporters of Congress; by the feeling that the quarrel was simply one between two groups of Englishmen, colonial and imperial, both of whom had been traditionally hated enemies of the French in Canada; and by resentment at the widespread pillaging to which the ill-supplied American forces resorted in the latter stages of their campaigning and retreat.*

---

* S. Ryerson, *The Founding of Canada Beginnings to 1815* (Toronto: Progress Books, 1960), pp. 210-215.

7 F. OUELLET (1966)
ROLES OF THE *ÉLITES TRADITIONNELLES*, THE *BOURGEOISIE* AND THE *HABITANTS*

Ouellet's Histoire économique *challenges many hitherto basic assumptions underlying Canadian historiography. His chapter on the Revolution and Quebec does not introduce any startling new hypothesis but rather brings together the work of various Twentieth Century historians, carefully filtered through an unusually incisive and imaginative mind. His analysis of the reaction of the* habitants *to the Americans is particularly impressive. Here is one historian who is concerned with viewing events through the eyes of contemporaries.*

The American Revolution posed a certain challenge to Canadians. An important part of the empire was dissociating itself from the rest, and making repeated appeals for liberty and independence. To what degree did this discordant voice influence public opinion in Quebec? The question has been asked on many occasions; some have said that the separatist attitudes of the peasants were being suppressed by the élite, while others have put the emphasis on the loyalty of the governing classes. Hence the affirmation has been repeated hundreds of times that British rule was saved by the French Canadians. In his study on Canada and the American Revolution, Marcel Trudel is the historian who has perhaps best recorded the oscillations of public opinion at this time. Nevertheless, it seems necessary, without hoping to exhaust the question, to study it by relating it, on the present occasion, to the general situation of that period in its entirety.

When the insurrection of the thirteen colonies broke out, not every social group was capable of clearly seeing its responsibilities, and of defining without the shadow of a doubt a firm line of conduct. Imperial solidarity was less an admitted fact than in 1760-65. Previous dissentions were still, in the eyes of many, present to such an extent that the idea of a sacred union against the enemy could not be a spontaneous phenomenon rallying the support of all. Besides, the Canadian economy, by reason of the insufficiency of its integration with the empire and the economic power of New England, was not as interdependent on England as it was later to become. It seems that on this point, the majority of historians have emphasized the effectiveness of an integration based on the fur trade alone. One can understand why the economic unrest and the social tensions of the preceding ten years had contributed in a sense to veil the profound community of interests which existed between the colony and the metropolis. Thus there arose among business circles a serious uncertainty regarding the prospects for the future. Again, in 1778—and that in spite of clarifications which have been brought to bear since the beginning of the hostilities—the fur traders were to retain some doubts on the practical validity of their options. 'Although this trade,' they wrote, 'is by far the most considerable in the province, since the beginning of the present rebellion, the difficulties are so alarming, that as soon as communications are reestablished with Albany, a large portion of this traffic will be carried on with the province of New York, even though the situation in Canada is more advantageous in many respects.' As far as one can see, complete unanimity did not exist in Quebec society on the eve of the American invasion. If the clergy and the nobility did not entertain any doubts on the nature of their duty, it cannot have been so with the bourgeoisie. With regard to the peasant classes, their attitude is equally comprehensible in this confusing situation. Carleton was shocked but did not try to understand. An unfavourable economic context, social contentions,—such are the factors which prevented the different social groups from feeling as strongly as they would have under other circumstances the call of certain values, obvious ten years earlier, and even more obvious ten years after the revolutionary phenomenon.

The *Quebec Act*, a logical outcome of an evolution begun in 1766, consolidated into a coherent policy the views of Murray and Carleton. As a result, it dissipated the haze which still hovered over the future of Quebec. The numerical superiority of the French-Canadians, a phenomenon which appeared irreversible then, demanded, in the eyes of British leaders, the maintenance not only of their local customs, but of their social structures as well. Hence it was necessary to build the future by relying on the traditional élites: the clergy and the seigneurs. As for the bourgeoisie, nothing seemed to indicate, in the economic context and still less in the demographic equilibrium, that it might soon reach the status of a governing class. . . .

Thus Carleton had only to congratulate himself on the attitude and conduct of the clergy and the nobility. In 1775, Cramahé wrote: 'But justice must be done to the nobility, the clergy, and the greater part of the bourgeoisie, who have given great proof of zeal and fidelity to service, and have made great efforts to make the infatuated peasants listen to reason. . . .' Two years later, Carleton expressed the same point of view: 'In the troubled times which we are going through, the nobility, the clergy and the greater part of the bourgeoisie have given the government every possible support, and their efforts are going to contribute greatly to reestablish that spirit of subordination without which rules have no effect.' Regarding the behaviour of these two governing classes, clerics and seigneurs, there is no possible doubt. Everything summoned them to an indefectible solidarity with the established order and the empire. Some people have led us to believe that the *Quebec Act* alone, by the immediate advantages which it provided for these two groups, was responsible for their support of British rule. To accept this interpretation as a whole is to misunderstand the ideological basis of their relationship with the established government. Behind the options of the seigneurs and the members of the clergy there is not only the consideration of more or less special interests, but also the obedience to values accepted without qualification. To evaluate the positions adopted by the clergy and the nobles in the light of contemporary nationalistic values would be to speak a language which the men of that time did not understand, and to distort their vision of reality.

In 1774, everything united the clergy and seigneurs to the government. The belief in absolute monarchy and divine right took on an even greater significance since the bourgeoisie was now demanding parliamentary government and proposing its own system of values. Loyalty to the king, being based on the religious convictions of these two social groups, remained the strongest sentiment. Therefore, simply because of the basic adhesions of this élite, there could be no question of its rising up against England. The principle of the union of Church and State was another incontestable credo which united the clergy to the political status quo. As for the nobility, it had always considered military activity as one of its essential social functions. The duty of defending the country was incumbent on it more than on any other class. In any case, were the values proposed by the rebels acceptable? Condemnable in principle, the Revolution aimed moreover at breaking the traditional political relationships. The rebels invoked the theme of liberty, whereas, the French-Canadian élite believed in authority, in obedience, and in aristocratic values.

The situation might have been different if British policy after 1763 had threatened the social and economical position of the Church and hindered its action in the domain of religion. But on the contrary, the situation of the Church had continued to improve, and the *Quebec Act* actually conferred on it a privileged status by recognizing its right to collect the tithe and assuring its basic source of wealth. The governors had doubtless exercised a certain control over the clergy, but their interventions hardly overstepped the boundaries traced by Gallic precepts. Even the English Catholic had to wait for more than fifty years before obtaining guarantees equally as complete. Therefore it is not surprising that Monseigneur Briand, from the very beginning of the conflict, intervened in order to remind his flock of its obligations, and to advise its members to take part in the conflict on the side of the established order. The Bishop of Quebec was not content merely to affirm principles, but even outlined the penalties in store for those who violated their oath of allegiance.

On the other hand, the *Quebec Act* filled the seigneurs with great hopes. The reestablishment of French civil law, the maintenance of the seigneurial system, the abolition of the oath of the Test as well as the refusal of an Assembly, strengthened their conviction that they were going to recover all their former privileges and at the same time get the bourgeoisie out of the way. In the spring of 1775, the American J. Brown wrote:

> The French-Canadians are the kind of people who know no other way of procuring riches and honour for themselves other than by becoming court sycophants; and since the inauguration of French laws is going to give positions to the lesser French nobility, they are crowding around the governor. . . .

From then on their arrogance knew no bounds. They realized that the military situation gave them a special prominence which the bourgeoisie had no means of combatting. Punctilious to a degree, they surpassed the British soldiery in attachment to the monarchy. There was only one weak point in this armour: the war revealed the exact measure of their influence on the people. However, the new constitution promised them sinecures and economic advantages. Judge Hey said the following on this subject:

> On the other hand, these men [the seigneurs] are too proud and are priding themselves far too greatly upon the advantages which they hope to receive from the restoration of their former privileges and customs, and on this account, they allow themselves reflections and remarks designed to wound not only the Canadians [the peasants and the merchants] but the English merchants as well. The scanty relationship which I had with them on the Council gave me no indication of any ability or moderation on their part; they yield to no argument, however strong or just it may be, and they refuse to consent to any modification of their previous laws, especially regarding commercial matters. I insist on the need to make some changes in this regard in order to favour the English merchants, to whom we owe almost all the commerce which is carried on in the province, and without whom this province, except for a few articles produced in small quantities, would become in short a non-commercial colony. . . .

The intransigence and the pretentions of the seigneurs added to their economic weakness, are obvious signs of a social decline which was not to be made clear until the day when the military situation would no longer justify part of their role in society. Excessive attachment of their privileges, to tradition, contempt for the tradespeople, a change of attitude regarding the tenant-farmers—these are the factors responsible for a lack of prestige already initiated at the economic level. It was in vain that they increased the rates of payment in kind and the rents, for they did not succeed in adjusting their income to their style of living; it was in vain that they tried to guild their coat of arms with sinecures and wealthy marriages, for they did not stave off an irreparable decadence. Henceforward the governors were no longer to say: 'The seigneurs exercise a profound influence on the people,' but rather: 'The seigneurs claim to exercise. . . .' The nuance is fundamental.

Regarding the bourgeoisie, one can easily understand the uncertainties of its position at the moment of the revolutionary explosion. In almost every field it had collided with the competition of New England. In the colony, the governors instead of taking into consideration their opinions and their just claims, had endeavoured to maintain the merchants in a state of political subordination which appeared unacceptable to people who were British subjects by birth. Hence their social role had been progressively reduced in accordance with their numerical importance, whereas their economic power would have justified a more flexible attitude. Then came the *Quebec Act* which crystallized everything, and took away their English Civil law, their English commercial rights, trial by jury and *habeas corpus*. Carleton even spoke of restoring French criminal law, since it was understood that English criminal law favoured the insolence of the individual, whereas the other system would be more favourable to subordination. The legislation of 1774 even rejected the parliamentary system. Shall one be astonished, then, that a few merchants at the beginning seriously considered the American point of view, and that some actually finished by adopting it? The majority of the merchants however, quickly realized the advantages which the new situation promised. Besides, the revolution accelerated a revival of contact with certain values, such as British liberty, which had always been deeply rooted in them in spite of its momentary setback. Even if, in 1775-76, many *bourgeois* took up arms to assure the defence of the country, the majority no less continued throughout the revolutionary period to attend to their businesses. It was for economic reasons that they laboured to promote a Canadian identity henceforth united to England. Concerning the internal reforms which they advocated, the trading classes determined to obtain them by different methods than those used in the past. Up until then, business circles had been satisfied merely to make requests of the king, with the London merchants backing them up. In 1777, they modified their strategy. The establishment of a Chamber of Commerce helped to compensate for the absence of parliamentary institutions and gave them more weight in the metropolis. Shortt wrote:

> To escape the commercial disabilities of the restored French law a plan was devised and advocated, first in the town of Quebec and afterwards in Montreal, for the establishment of Chambers of Commerce for these towns and adjoining districts. In 1777 Governor Carleton submitted the Quebec proposal to the British Government. The Chamber of Commerce was to be composed of all merchants and traders of both races in Quebec. It was to be managed by twenty-five

> directors, including a president and other officers, these to be elected annually, five to constitute a quorum. The board of directors, or a quorum of them, was to constitute a board of arbitrators to decide such commercial matters in dispute as might be brought them. The decision of the board was to be final in all actions not exceeding 50 pounds. Beyond that amount there might be an appeal to the full board, with a quorum of at least, thirteen members, the decision of this larger board to be final for all amounts. The directors were to have power to frame rules and regulations for the general benefit of trade, subject to the approval of the whole body of members. These rules should be laid before the government of the province, and, if approved, should pass into law. . . .

As for the peasants, they chose neutrality much to the shock of the governor and of the élite. Cramahé wrote: 'Every means has been attempted without success to make the Canadian peasant aware of his duty and to engage him to take up arms for the defence of the province.' In May, 1777 Carleton stated: 'There is no doubt that it is possible to reduce the Canadians to the state of deference and obedience in which they were held under the former government, although this can only be brought about in time.' How are we to explain the fact that the habitants, still imbued with the ideal of monarchy and with the feeling of fidelity to the king, and so little inclined to the revolutionary ideology, adopted and held an attitude of neutrality and passiveness in the conflict? In August 1775, Judge Hey posed the problem in these terms:

> Nevertheless I am sometimes led to believe that these people are neither ungrateful nor rebellious and that the ruses and assidiousness of the agents of some of the colonies who spent last winter here got the better of these people whose fear is joined to an ignorance and a credulity which are difficult to imagine. Perhaps it is still possible to re-awaken their consciousness of their duty and of their true interests by being moderate on their behalf, and by using methods designed to persuade them and to instruct them; and when the Canadians understand that the danger consists of remaining impassive at the present time, and of refusing to prepare for defence, they will take up arms not only to defend themselves in the actual moment, but, if they are supported by the King's troops, they will even be willing to take part in any offensive manoeuver.

In reality, the reaction of the peasants appears much more complex than was believed at the time. It is certain that the impotence and lack of military preparation of the government deprived the habitant of his sense of security and engendered a reflex of fear. At St-Jean, Carleton could count on only 500 soldiers. It must also be said that the revolutionary propaganda deeply exploited the fear of the peasants and filled them with new anxieties. The habitant soon became convinced that the English government only wanted to enroll him in order to organize all the better a mass deportation. This feeling seems to have been a natural adjunct of the peasants' mistrust. In 1760, they demanded guarantees against deportation; in 1763, on the occasion of Pontiac's rebellion, the habitant hesitated at first to enlist out of fear of being deported; in 1775, this feeling rose to the surface, consolidating the passiveness of the habitant. Judge Hey took these views into account: 'Some of them believe that they have been sold to the Spaniards (whom they abhor) and that general Carleton has already received payment for them. In short, I do not believe that men have ever been seen prey to such a confusion of ignorance, fear, credulity, perversion, and prejudice, which, in the circumstances, renders our conduct in their regard so difficult.'

The neutrality of the peasants had other sources equally as effective. One must not forget that war had been an almost permanent occupation of the habitant of New France: one could say that he was a perpetual conscript. The nobility aside, the Canadians had felt that the surrender was for them the inauguration of a period of perpetual peace. They had had enough of war. The conqueror, so they believed, in taking away their arms, had agreed to take up the defence of the territory. But at the moment when the Seven Years' War was officially coming to a close, another conflict loomed up in the west. Pontiac's conspiracy, by initiating voluntary enlistment and the system of remuneration for enlisted men, gave a new meaning to the military activity of the habitant. The establishment of the system of voluntary military service in 1763, placed the principle of *loyalty to the king* in a new perspective. In the final instance, voluntary military service provided a place for the option of neutrality. Military service, a strict obligation during the French period, was to become in the future a matter of free choice for the individual. However, the growing agitation in New England, and the views of Carleton as well as those of the élite, tended to bring military activity back to its traditional dimensions. But the system of voluntary military service, once it had penetrated the peasant mentality, would not be easily abandoned. Between the self-interest of the individual and the expression of his feeling of loyalty, there was to be much freedom of choice. It is because they underestimated the importance of this change issuing from British rule, that the governors, and after them, the historians, were to misinterpret the behavior of the peasant masses during the American Revolution. Hence the importance, for the comprehension of the oscillations of public opinion, of a precise analysis of the economic situation before and during the revolutionary phenomenon. It is certain that pre-war economic difficulties and social tensions were an important cause of instability, at least among the peasant classes. On the other hand, it is clear that the series of good harvests, between 1770 and 1778, influenced the habitant's decision to the highest degree. By staying on his farm, the cultivator was certain to be able to reap some fine *écus*, along with his wheat. This explains the following judgment of Carleton: 'There are some of them who are guided by feelings of honour, but the majority are influenced only by the lure of gain or by the fear of punishment.' After having for a long time paid in the end the expenses of military operations, and having looked on, powerless, while the speculators enriched themselves, the peasants seem this time to have been determined to seize the opportunity which was being presented. The image of the *Great Society* and of its vexations measures were present in the minds of all. They had supplied the population of Quebec and the English army with provisions, but when the invader offered cash for their produce, they were incapable of resisting. But the day when the Americans flaunted paper money, the habitant was dismayed; he hid his wheat and forced the enemy to make requisitions. From then on, the peasant classes did not hide their hostility. The general neutrality of the rural areas should not induce us to postulate a movement of defection among the masses. There was doubtless a certain receptiveness to revolutionary propaganda in a few places, but, on the whole, the French-Canadian rural society remained loyal to British rule. The passiveness of the habitant resulted from the lack of governmental military forces, from the manifold fears which assailed the peasant's mind, and from the consideration of economic interest.*

---

* F. Ouellet, *Histoire économique et sociale du Québec 1760-1850* (Montréal: Fides, 1966), pp. 116-124. Translated for this edition by George A. Rawlyk.

D. CRITICAL SUMMARY

In all probability, the two most satisfying answers to the question of why Quebec did not join the American Revolution are provided by A. L. Burt and F. Ouellet. Burt accurately pointed out the weakness of the American military thrust into Quebec as well as the strategic advantages of the British. Ouellet, on the other hand, showed why various groups in Quebec—the clergy, seigneurs, merchants, and habitants *decided not to join the invaders. The work of these two historians should be supplemented by Trudel's* Louis XVI, Le Congrès Américain et Le Canada 1774-1789, *Lanctôt's* Le Canada et La Révolution Américaine *and Neatby's* Quebec the Revolutionary Age 1760-1791.

In spite of the considerable work already done on Quebec and the American Revolution, much remains to be done. In certain respects, Professor Ouellet indicates a path that further research could profitably take. Specialized studies in considerable depth of the role of the habitants, *the seigneurs, the clergy and the merchants are needed. These studies should attempt to follow the vicissitudes in the thinking of these groups, especially during the early revolutionary years. Biographies of key individuals involved in Quebec during the Revolution, as well as sophisticated regional studies, should also be undertaken.*

Another problem deserving of examination is the extent to which the French Canadians desired to see Canada restored to French sovereignty and saw in the American invasion some hope of achieving this aim. In 1768 the French in Louisiana had risen in revolt against Spanish rule and Guy Carleton had been concerned lest a similar resistance movement, with French direction, should emerge in his province; indeed, one purpose of the Quebec Act had been to prevent this possible development. A study of this question is unlikely to provide much in the way of new and brilliant insights, but it might well help to illuminate some of the dark corners that still exist in our understanding of Quebec's role in the American Revolution, 1775-1776.